D1006908

EDUCATION AND THE US GOVERNMENT

At a time when central government control of education in many countries is growing rapidly, this book on the historical determinants of U.S. educational legislation is of great relevance. The book looks in detail at the history of the relationship between the U.S. Government and the provision of educational services. It assesses the contributions made to educational legislation by key political figures such as Franklin, Washington and Jefferson. The author also examines in depth the role of congress and the president, the relationship between the federal government and the state legislature and the role of the judiciary in education. An account of the hard-fought battle for the right to equal educational opportunities for the American Negro and the American Indian is of considerable interest. Finally, the book compares the American educational system with that of other countries.

Education and the US Government

Donald K. Sharpes

ST. MARTIN'S PRESS
New York

© 1987 Donald K. Sharpes

All rights reserved. For information, write:
Scholarly & Reference Division,
St. Martin's Press, Inc., 175 Fifth Avenue, New York, NY 10010
First published in the United States of America in 1987

Printed in Great Britain

Library of Congress Cataloging-in-Publication Data

Sharpes, Donald K.
   Education and the US Government.

   Includes index.
   1. Education — United States — History.
2. Education and State — United States. I. Title.
LA212.S48 1987   370′.973   86-29839
ISBN 0-312-00467-2

Contents

Part One: The Origins of Federal Education

Democracy does not confer the most skilful kind of government upon the people, but it produces that which the most skilful governments are frequently unable to awaken, namely, an all-pervading and restless activity, a super-abundant force, and an energy which is inseparable from it, and which may, under favorable circumstances, beget the most amazing benefits. These are the true advantages of democracy.

Alexis de Tocqueville

Introduction

Those who look in any such direction for the realization of their hopes leave out of the idea of good government its principal element, the improvement of the people themselves.

John Stuart Mill

Democracy in America—and the democratic governance of education—is qualitatively different, both as a political and governmental system, and as an influence for preserving freedoms, from any other political system in the world. Education sponsored, endorsed or adjudicated by the federal government, however, is a part of that democratic process. Federal education is often considered a collection of odd facts, changing programmes, and variable funding priorities. It is often looked upon as an exercise in questionable politics that varies with the party in power, or the tussle between parties. Such activities apparently have no bearing upon the governance or the process of education in states or local communities.

This view is erroneous. The principles and practices of the federal government in education actually illuminate a major elemental democratic force: the effect of the Constitution in our lives.

One of the three characteristics of Americans that Alexis de Tocqueville described is their potential to evolve into a 'tyranny of the majority'. The young aristocrat's journey in 1831 only confirms what we know today, that our feelings about government are ambivalent, forming a tension between love and hate, wanting what government gives, but resentful of it for giving it. John Stuart Mill described this tension as an 'antagonism of influences', and claimed it was the only security for continued progress.

Today many Americans believe this tyranny *is* 'big government'. But perhaps it is the supreme irony that the federal government, most notably in education, has prevented the domination of any one group, including the states, over education control.

Democracy does not mean letting state and local governments run their own affairs without federal participation. That, quite simply, is to ignore what the Constitution is — the creator of centralised, national government to protect individual rights and promote common interests and the 'general welfare'.

3

Understanding the federal government's role in education is thus understanding democracy in action. Informed intelligence about the democratic role of the federal government will never lead us to accept the myth that we can curtail centralised governmental functions without also eroding those liberties and freedoms we take for granted.

Political parties, federal executives and legislators will indeed differ on the precise role and emphasis the government should take in education. But the constitutional powers available to government to act educationally as it sees fit is a matter of historical record and becomes the central treatise of this book.

Democracy is still young in America. Our experience with federalism — the union of the states with the national government — is equally young compared with other countries.

The federal government does not need the states' co-operation to achieve its purposes, and can execute laws without them — indeed can override *their* laws. Individual citizens have direct access to the federal judiciary. This freedom of direct appeal to the federal courts has equalised the mechanism for achieving justice. But it has also centralised the governance of certain freedoms, and created bureaucracies for decision-making at the highest levels.

Although federal interference is anathema to some, the polls confirm that the general public does not understand elementary civics or the Constitution. It 'intrudes', it has too much power, and it over-regulates, to use a few of the popular phrases of complaint about 'big' government.

On the other hand, realisable benefits in our time have been the extension of voting rights and privileges, civil liberties and rights, and equality of educational opportunity. The active pursuit of social equality (including schooling) cannot occur without democratically controlled change brought about by centralised government, or violent revolution. Our history has been that local and state schooling has, in fact, impeded equality of schooling. Local and state schooling has in many cases only reflected social class differences in the communities.

One interest group follows another, sometimes in proportion to the political party in power (since they have a hand in the election process), and exerts its influence more ardently once positioned in a power base. The tensions occurring now for equal rights for women, abortion amendments, foreign policy, nuclear deterrence, all confirm de Tocqueville's prediction about potential 'tyranny of the majority'. Americans are called upon to know what government is legally permitted to do, what its limitations are, and the history of government life in fields like education.

Education issues, like other domestic-policy matters, become a part of public policy by a variety of approaches: political campaigns (Carter's promise to create a Department of Education; Reagan's promise to abolish it); influential citizens; government agencies; domestic disturbances (busing riots, assassinations, media documentaries); and the persistent lobbying of special education interest groups seeking preferential treatment. So what is, or what should be, the federal role in education? One of the premisses of this book is that the federal role in education is determined by the politics of the federal government at any given point in time. But it is also determined by the three different branches of government acting with constitutionally different powers. In a very real sense there have always been three distinct federal roles in education: executive, legislative and judicial. The federal role, then, is not limited to, or dominated by any one branch of government.

This study is not merely a history of education in America. Nor is it a description of federal programmes and policies. Quite a number of these studies exist already. Rather, it is to elaborate on two pivotal concepts: that there is and always has been a federal role in American education; and that it is intrinsically a part of the democratic process and has been since the Constitution was formed and the republic founded.

It is more pertinent to point, not to the federal government's derived powers on behalf of education, but to the bureaucracies it has created to carry out its functions. Some federal agencies, like that created by the Federal Election Campaign Act of 1974, have combined all the powers of government itself — executive, legislative and judicial. Some, like the Federal Bureau of Investigation (FBI) under J. Edgar Hoover, are a pure reflection of their chief. Others, like the Central Intelligence Agency (CIA), are run by the specialists and professionals. Yet others, like the Department of Education, serve at the political caprice of the President and the Congress.

Bureaucratic government in a democracy may well be considered a necessary evil. But the challenge to democratic federal involvement in education is to purify the bureaucracies of some of the laws governing them, and to limit the scope of their execution.

It is my belief that the role of the federal government in education is *democratic*, that is, subject to the pressures of the body politic, from special interest groups including educators. But that role is also *constitutional*, in that the federal government's power is explicit and

5

inherent in the powers of the Constitution. The federal role in education is also in the tradition of *federalism*: a shared partnership with state authorities, yet separate and distinct from them.

A brief definition of each of these key terms is in order. I define *democracy* as that form of government which permits participation of a people through constitutional powers they possess implicitly. Governments are created to assist the people in ordering their collective lives, and to protect their powers. The Declaration of Independence says that to secure these rights, 'governments are instituted amongst men, deriving their just powers from the consent of the governed'.

I define *politics* as the legitimate exercise of a constitutionally free people in governing themselves, either singly or in groups.

I define the role of the federal government in education to be *constitutionally* valid based on the powers conferred on the respective branches by the Constitution. The federal government does operate schools, colleges and educational systems and establishments (as we shall see later); Congress has the right to pass legislation of any kind affecting the public good; federal courts can interpret the Constitution that expands or limits based on law, the kind of schooling individuals receive.

I define *federalism* as the mutual sharing of the powers resident in the Constitution, and in the people, among national and state governments. The Constitution confers powers to a federal, a national government, and asks the states to share their power to make it work. It would not be far-fetched to claim that the ambiguous nature of this relationship and sharing of powers has been used by politicians of all persuasions as the central theme of their political campaigns: they run against Washington (both Carter and Reagan did), or against the federal government, or against the 'encroachments' of state government. Garry Wills (1978) notes:

> It [the Constitution] created new powers, not so much over individuals as over these old loci of power, the states. Indeed, the main task was to get those old centers to surrender certain prerogatives; and the effort at reassuring them led to lingering ambiguities in our use of the very term 'federalism'.

One of the reasons I believe that education was not specifically mentioned in the Constitution (although the phrase 'to promote the progress of Science and the useful arts' could be so interpreted) was not because it was a forgotten or neglected topic. Indeed, education was frequently in the writings of the principal designers of the republic. It was because, in the latter half of the eighteenth century, education was too closely identified with religious instruction. At that time there was no common school tradition, and it would have been politically and ideologically incompatible to promote religious schooling. The major participants in the drama that created the democracy all thought too highly of education to have purposely excluded it without political cause.

I am not among those who believe that the federal government infringes on local control of schools. There are of course instances of inordinate and excessive administrative work associated with the acceptance of federal funds. Local authorities are not bound, for example, by the same constitutional obligations for protecting individual freedoms as is the federal government. Educators, and the general public, have not fully accepted the statutory responsibilities of the federal government in education as they have, say, in transportation, air traffic, agriculture, housing, and health. Our view of the role of federalism in education should not result from lack of understanding the Constitution, the tradition of law in education, or the historical precedents that have all guided how we have educated our people.

The Reagan Administration's 1982 Budget Request makes this point about policy direction:

Education policy has historically been the prerogative of State and local authorities. In recent years, the Federal government has become increasingly involved in this non-Federal responsibility. The Administration proposes to shift control over education policy from the Federal Government to State and local authorities.

There is no doubt that the federal involvement in education has expanded dramatically, yet the growth of educational programmes in education has not meant less control. The federal government has not taken power away from public schools; it has in fact added to programmes that were in many instances non-existent in local schools. Education is, and always has been, a matter of federal concern and responsibility.

Moreover, the expansion of federal programmes in education from 1964 to 1981, although unprecedented in size and number, was not basically a sudden and radical departure from the history of the federal government's commitment to education. In fact, as we shall see in Part I, the origins of that commitment and role stretch back to the

7

founding of the republic. If a democracy depends on a population enlightened and educated, especially about is government, then our knowledge of how the federal government works on behalf of education can only strengthen our belief in the ultimate survival of both education and government.

A careful scrutiny of government, from what ever vantage point, is always in order. Active knowledge about government is the first requisite of an enlightened citizenry. I have used the historical approach in this study, because history reveals just how much a part of our past we are. History reveals truths that illuminate our present conditions.

I do not presume to be able to foretell what will be future federal government policy in education; but I am confident from this domestic-sector analysis that it will build on past precedents, and be supplemental to, and often connective of local schooling. Some may believe that the federal government should have no role in education; yet the present evidence is that it has been actively involved since the origins of American democracy and prominent in the writing of the founders.

One of the avowed purposes of the constitution framers was to have citizens knowledgeable about government itself, as a hedge against potential totalitarian abuses. That policy is now in acute disarray as evidence accumulates that students and teachers alike are more ignorant than past generations of what government is, how it operates, what its limits are. There is more than nominal ignorance about the three branches of government and their respective powers.

The bandying-about of political slogans often clouds the public conception of the function of national government. Each generation must relearn the civic lessons that led to the formation of rational government, that new kind of government in partnership with independent states. This study forms a part of that process of educating for democratic understanding.

1

Education in the Confederacy and in the Constitution

It is difficult to understand the relationship between federal and state government in education unless we can somewhat faithfully reconstruct the fundamental concepts that prevailed among the moulders of the documents now guiding our governmental activities.

As the Declaration of Independence notes, the British king had 'a history of repeated inquiries and usurpations, all having in direct object, the establishment of an absolute tyranny over these States'. It was thus predictable for the states to eclipse the power of the executive in government. Ten states had governors serving only a one-year term, and Pennsylvania had no governor at all.

But if a king was not in charge, who then? The literate and knowledgeable men of the times turned to the political philosophers, as Garry Wills (1978) so adroitly documents: Hume, Locke, the Scottish Enlightenment.

The central idea was 'popular sovereignty'. It was to surface again in the late 1850s and early 1860s on behalf of the states' rights to maintain slavery. But it meant that the people everywhere were the source of governmental power.

The Georgia State Constitution in 1777 declared:

> We, therefore, the representatives of the people, from whom all power originates and for whose benefit all government is intended, by virtue of the power delegated to us, do ordain . . . that the following rules and regulations be adopted for the future government of this state.

In most states the representatives of the people, delegates to the legislature, elected the governor, judges and all other officers of the state government. The governor or chief executive did not have appointive power over his officers. These legislatures were the heirs to the colonial parliaments.

9

Limited government, an idea that has some popularity today, was in vogue in the late 1770s; but because states could not agree among themselves, nor allow the union to arbitrate their disputes, each state became an authoritarian island unto itself. The Articles of Confederation were an attempt to form a more workable political union.

THE ARTICLES OF CONFEDERATION

It was not ethereal philosophies of democracy and political forms of government that led to a unification of the 13 independent states. It was mercantile and economic circumstances, and the war with England. Inflation and insolvency were paramount issues, and although most Americans living in the early 1780s were not immediately touched by the war, everyone's earthly goods were in potential jeopardy.

What the band of merchants, bankers and others wanted was to establish a rational political structure that would solidify credit abroad, free it from the vagaries of state legislatures, and impose a uniform tax structure. Only a unified political federation could rescue credit overseas and help expand commerce and trade. So a unique form of political union arose from fears of public debt. It is often the unintended consequences that are more significant over time than the contemporary issues.

> Dissatisfaction with the existing political order was most prevalent in the propertied class, but by 1780 the idea of strengthening the central government was supported by a considerable and diversified body of opinion. Four years before, this would have been unthinkable.
>
> (Ferguson and McHenry, 1950)

What would the states do, having gained independence, still fighting a war up and down its east coast, to maintain their sense of unity — political, social and financial? Article II declared: 'Each state retains its sovereignty, freedom and independence, and every power, jurisdiction and right, which is not by this confederation expressly delegated to the United States, in Congress assembled.' There was no political relinquishment of power at all, and this was, after the title, the first sentence of the Articles. The Articles were meant to strengthen the independence of the states, especially some of the smaller ones, but not at the expense of the potential disintegration of the loose confederation between them. The Articles formalised the union, but constituted primarily a legal partnership based on mutual trust and understanding.

This was not the formation of a national government. There was a common treasury to help defray the war costs. The delegates were appointed by the state legislatures, and no state could make war or treaties without the consent of the Continental Congress. There was no executive and no judiciary. But most important, there was no *taxing* authority, and no method for regulating commerce between the states.

The principal purpose of the confederated union was to form a common defence against enemies — Spain and France still had claims in the New World — which might challenge the independent states militarily. Article III applies:

> The said states hereby severally enter into a firm league of friendship with each other, for their common defense, the security of their liberties, and mutual and general welfare, binding themselves to assist each other, against all force offered to, or attacks made upon them or any of them, on account of religion, sovereignty, trade, or any other pretence whatsoever.

It was like a contract between gentlemen, with no binding sanctions possible, no coercion, no arbitration if there were violations.

And what about the rights of individual citizens? The Articles contain very little, but certain phrases have been retained in the Constitution and its amendments. The 'privileges and immunities' clause is especially noteworthy:

> The better to secure and perpetuate mutual friendship and intercourse among the people of the different states in this Union, the free inhabitants of each of these states, paupers, vagabonds and fugitives excepted, shall be entitled to all privileges and immunities of free citizens in the several states.

The purpose of the statement was to protect merchants and traders and to encourage commerce. But who were those that were excluded — the paupers, vagabonds and fugitives? And those not free? They had no privileges. How many citizens were thus deprived of their rights in the days following independence? To find out we must add those who were poor and in debt, those without land, the wanderers (those later would build the West), those in flight because of actual or alleged crimes, and those in bondage: perhaps 30 per cent of the actual population of the 1780s.

Even though there was a clear distinction between those who were and those who were not entitled to privileges under the Articles, an attempt was made to secure Canada's entry into the confederation. Canada's refusal to join was a disappointment. That nation, however, was later to prove a safe refuge for east coast Indians, especially those from Virginia, when the Civil War broke out and they did not wish to take sides in the conflict.

'Vagabonds' were very likely those who had been indentured, a rare breed sold first to the captain of the vessel, and then to whomsoever might purchase him or her to work off servitude over a set number of years. It was the manner in which most of the colonies were populated. Lack of food supplies forced the Puritans to release many of their number to wander, as they did when Salem was low on its luck in 1630.

By the time of Independence and the union of the colonies there were thousands of formerly indentured and masterless men and families. The indenture system needed manpower to put the raw resources of the colonies to work. Carrying human cargo was extra money for ship owners whose hardware and textiles westbound to the colonies were usually lighter and thus could accommodate more space than the heavier and bulkier sugar, molasses and tobacco on the return voyage. Counted as cargo, there were no questions asked about the qualifications of the 'paupers' journeying to the yeoman's work in the colonies. Tobacco growers would pay eight to ten pounds for such a man to reach them alive. Thirteen of the 30 members of Virginia's House of Burgesses in 1633 are known to have landed with their passage paid for by others.

Convicted and forced exiles of the European nations also became the nation's new stock. Thirty thousand convicts alone, perhaps a third of them women, were put ashore by unscrupulous captains between 1713 and 1775, roughly 4 per cent of all immigrants, mostly disembarked in Maryland and Virginia. Benjamin Franklin suggested that return boatloads of rattlesnakes would repay the Mother Country's generosity. When the Union finally passed a law forbidding the landing of convicts in the newly independent colonies, England began shipping them to Australia.

The Reverend Jonathan Boucher guessed that perhaps two-thirds of the schooling in Virginia — one must believe in the other colonies as well — originated from 'indentured servants or transported felons. Not a ship arrives . . . with . . . convicts in which schoolmasters were not as regularly advertised for sale as . . . any other trade'. Given the circumstances surrounding Abraham Lincoln's birth, it is likely that his stock came from indentured servants and convicts.

However, there were those who were not indentured and who were not safeguarded by the 'custom of the country' because they had no contracts at all prior to their ship's departure. The high visibility of the black prevented him from becoming a 'vagabond', able to disappear in the colonies. The race barriers erected throughout all social life, cultivated from early childhood, were, like mortar holding stone, exceedingly slow to crumble.

Blacks were not the only slaves. South Carolina in 1709 had 2,400 adult white, 2,900 Negro and 1,100 adult Indian slaves. Many Indian tribes were as mercenary as the speculators and ships' captains bartering white human cargo. Declaring war on neighbouring tribes and capturing prisoners was economically profitable. It also inevitably led to tribal suicide by decimating the southeast Indian tribes of their hardier inhabitants.

No one knew at the time of the Articles that America was destined to be democratic and egalitarian — in its written ideals at least. The Articles of Confederation were not framed without opposition. The Galloway Plan, proposed by the conservatives in the First Continental Congress who hoped to avoid independence from Britain, provided for an American parliament operating in tandem with the British parliament, similar to the way the House and Senate are together in legislation. The radical party defeated this measure and even obliterated it from congressional journals. The conservatives managed to agree to a compromise that would permit the drafting of a document describing a federal government of the states. A committee to draft the Articles of Confederation was created on the same day in June 1776 that a committee was also established to write a Declaration of Independence. John Dickenson of Delaware, a leading opponent of independence, was primarily responsible for the Articles, and it was he who became the chief supporter of a strong central government. It can be said without reservation that he is the father of federalism.

Having denied the British government control over their destinies, states were not easily willing to yield their independence to an untested national government. The conservatives, those who wanted a strong central government, were again denied by the radicals who ensured that the Articles were federal, a partnership between the states. In fact, Thomas Burke of North Carolina, one of the radical leaders advocating sovereignty for the states, saw to it that a statement was retained that all powers not expressly delegated to the new government were held by the states. He can be said to be one of the fathers of sovereign states' rights.

Thus the advocates of a strong national and central government, the conservatives of their day, were temporarily defeated by the Articles of Confederation. However, by 1781 elections in the several states insured a radical majority in Congress. They were helped in their campaigns by the collapse of paper currency and the movement of the British troops northward from South Carolina (Charleston fell in 1780). New York in 1782, George Washington as commander-in-chief in 1783, Massachusetts in 1785, and Virginia in 1786, had all called for a new convention. Finally, Daniel Shay's rebellion ignited the fire for constitutional reform.

Money was the critical factor. Seven states had issued paper currency; others had established loan offices for the relief of debtors and taxpayers alike. But Massachusetts had refused this kind of aid, and Shay's rebellion was the result. Many states were in arrears to the Congress, which had no power to collect, and no authority over the states. The fact that the war was not over until October 1781 served to catalyse the forces to create a stronger government.

Some said anarchy would follow if the Articles were not amended. Others, like Elbridge Gerry of Massachusetts, feared civil war if a new constitution was ratified. Plenty of patriots were altogether opposed — George Mason (because there was no bill of rights), Edmund Randolph and Richard Henry Lee, all of Virginia.

From Independence until the Constitution, the rights of the colonists were the rights of the states exclusively. State sovereignty replaced the sovereignty of the king and colonial governor. The Articles of Confederation were in effect for only eight years (the document was written in 1777, but until 1781 only a minority of the states had signed) and it was to prove inadequate. Some of its essential issues still remain: should the central government be strictly federal, and have only delegated and limiting powers with sovereignty retained by the states, or should it be flexibly responsive government, not inhibited by any sovereign rights, except perhaps its own, and only loosely constrained by constitutional authority?

It has to be remembered that in the early 1780s there were no guarantees on individual liberties or protections of citizen freedoms against whatever states wished to impose. The Articles therefore reflect those recently independent states' concerns. Yet they are more than that. They are the union's first attempts at a central form of government to correct the problems individual states were not themselves able to resolve. Consequently, the roots of federalism, the relationship between national and state government regarding education, civil rights, or any other domestic social need, are in this era. It was a critical turning-point in American history. The document itself merits considerable more study than historians have given it.

When we consider a few of the central issues facing contemporary schooling — race, desegregation, student rights, social class, the relationship of property and property tax to education, and judge whether these are local, state or national problems, or any combination of these — the history of the formation of political relationships 200 years ago assumes a new stature.

EDUCATION AND THE WESTERN LANDS ISSUE

Irving Brant (1965) observes in his biography of James Madison:

Had dynamite been invented a century earlier, the issue of the western lands would have been filled with it. For a dozen years, after 1775, they furnished the source of bitterest contention among the states, producing alignments which had a lasting effect upon the structure of American government.

The claimed and unclaimed and counter-claimed Western lands — generally west of the Appalachian mountains, the dividing line of Revolutionary settlements — may appear at first to be misplaced in a study of the federal government and education. However, the subject is relevant because from the Continental Congress's attempts to settle the volatile land problems came some of the first federal laws pertaining to education.

The Western lands, their use, settlement and defence, had both singular potential advantages as well as grave dangers for the emerging nation. The advantages favoured the speculator, the settler who would cultivate the land, the minerals-seeker and the exploiter. The dangers, on the other hand, were equally obvious: possible war with France; war again with Britain (stirring up trouble for the newly independent colonies); war with Spain; war with American Indian tribes; war among the states themselves many of whom had rival claims on the abundant land. The British attempted to exploit this American weakness, a failure of complete unity, by sending spies to incite the Indians against frontier settlements.

The principle of primogeniture entail, whereby the eldest son inherited all the father's land, never became a popular custom throughout the colonies, although it was strongest in Virginia. In the colonial period large tracts were given to titled nobility in the 'new world' who were not first-born sons in England. The Fairfax Proprietary, for example, was granted by Charles in 1669 after much of the colony had already been settled. It comprised a tidy five million acres.

Against all these imported arguments about who should own the land stood the original natives. American Indians could never understand how anyone could 'own' Mother Earth.

From the British viewpoint, and with much justification, the Stamp Act — the insidious act which flamed into revolution — was simply a means of taxing defences for the Western lands. After Independence, the question of who was responsible for defence along the Western frontier became a singularly powerful political dilemma. So the Stamp Act, illustrated in history books as a raid on American wallets to fill British coffers, actually had as its purpose the legitimate defence of Western lands. The Stamp Act became the rallying point for the dissident forces favouring independence, including those much in debt to England for the purchase on loan of British manufactured goods. The gain to these political and mercantile forces was the cancellation of British debts. But independence did not make the land problem disappear. Seven of the 13 states claimed some or all of the Western lands, some because of their colonial charters. Many of the states — New York, Maryland, Virginia — had to cede their Western land claims in order to break the deadlock so that the confederacy could be born.

The Congress of the Confederation passed two major land ordinances: the Ordinance of Congress on Public Lands (1785), and the Northwest Ordinance (1787). Land speculators had offered Congress money for unsurveyed land, and Congress, desperately short of money because of the lingering and extensive war with Britain, could not resist the bait. The Ordinance of Congress on Public Lands declares: 'There shall be reserved the lot No. 16, of every township [a township was six miles square], for the maintenance of public schools within the said township.' Here is the federal government directing that schools be established, and even specifying exactly where, according to the surveyor's code, the maintenance money for schools shall be derived.

Two years later in the Northwest Ordinance of 1787, Article III, we find this arresting passage: 'Religion, morality, and knowledge, being necessary to good government and the happiness of mankind, schools and the means of education shall forever be encouraged.' This enabling legislation does not have the force of law with actual appropriated funds behind it, but it is an example of the legislative thinking of Congress to provide for education as a part of its responsibility. The territories along the west during this period were not states; these crucial documents, anticipating the Constitution (in the case of the Northwest Ordinance by only a few months) enjoined schooling only in those lands over which it had jurisdiction. These prerogatives themselves, even granted that education is omitted from the Constitution, forever set the precedent of the jurisdictional responsibility of the federal government to provide for schools and for education. These documents have the force of constitutional law. Furthermore, they came forth at a time that was extremely delicate for the untested union: the problems of the strength of the union itself; the doubtful war along the coast with Britain; potential wars along the western perimeters; Indian and French raids; navigational rights along rivers; states' disputes over land claims. Yet through it all, education was not a neglected domestic responsibility.

The fact that education is not specifically listed in the Constitution as an enumerated power seems less surprising, given the evidence of the importance accorded it in other legislation. Education is here, as it will be in a later time, spoken of in relation to national security and the general welfare. Robert Koenig (1978) agrees:

The Constitution makes no explicit reference to education. This does not mean, however, that education is beyond the purview of the federal government or is the exclusive function of the states. Early justification in legal theory for the intrusion of the federal government into education was based on the interpretation given to the general welfare clause of the Constitution.

THE TENTH AMENDMENT TO THE CONSTITUTION

They may think we are not sincere in our desire to incorporate such amendments in the Constitution as will secure those rights, which they consider as not sufficiently guarded.

That the people have an indubitable, unalienable and indefeasible right to reform or change their Government, whenever it be found adverse or inadequate to the purpose of its institutions.

Annals of Congress, May 1789

The authority for exclusive control of education by states, say some scholars and pundits, exists in the tenth amendment to the Constitution: 'The powers not delegated to the United States, but the Constitution, nor prohibited by it to the states, are reserved to the states respectively, or to the people'.

The Tenth Amendment, not originally a part of the document ratified establishing the national government, was added to pacify the radical group led by Thomas Burke of North Carolina. It was thus a political compromise aimed at calming the fears of southern states that the national government might usurp some of their established rights. The phrase, 'or to the people' meant the *vehicle of representation through the national government*, and not by means of some amorphous majority plebiscite.

The Tenth Amendment neither added to nor detracted from the original Constitution as ratified. This is evident from the discussion proceedings of James Madison when the amendment was pending. He said then:

> Interference with the power of the states was no constitutional criterion of the power of Congress. If the power was not given, Congress could not exercise it; if given, they might exercise it, although it should interfere with the laws or even the constitutions of the States.

What Madison said in a private letter to the influential Edmund Randolph is also significant to his thinking as the discussion over the Constitution was proceeding:

> I hold it for a fundamental point, that an individual independence of the States is utterly irreconcilable with the idea of an aggregate sovereignty. I think, at the same time, that a consolidation of the States into a simple republic is not less unattainable than it would be inexpedient. Let it be tried then whether any middle ground can be taken, which will at once support a due supremacy of the national authority, and leave in force the local authorities so far as they can be subordinately useful.

This passage seems to indicate, at least for Madison, that powers granted to states in no way constrained the powers of Congress; nor was there any sense of exclusivity: that is, that *only* states had rights to certain functions which the national government did not have.

However, from the death of John Marshall until the F.D. Roosevelt Administration, the Tenth Amendment was invoked by states in order to *curtail* powers expressly granted Congress. Chief Justice Stone rejected the Tenth Amendment as a claim for limiting federal powers:

> The power of Congress . . . is complete in itself, may be exercised to its fullest extent, and acknowledges no limitations other than are prescribed in the Constitution . . . that power can neither be enlarged nor diminished by the exercise or non-exercise of state power . . . Our conclusion is unaffected by the Tenth Amendment which . . . states but a truism that all is retained which has not been surrendered.

It is apparent from other documents and court decisions that the authority granted the federal government by the Constitution does not shield the states or any other political subdivisions from that authority. Justice Holmes noted in a case concerning interstate commerce: 'There is no question that this power (of the federal government) is superior to that of the states to provide for the welfare and necessities of their inhabitants.' (1925)

THE 'GENERAL WELFARE' CLAUSE

'We the People of the United States, in order to . . . promote the general welfare . . .' The phrase 'general welfare' also found in the Articles of Confederation, is contained in the Preamble to the Constitution: 'The Congress shall have the Power to lay and collect Taxes . . . and provide for the common Defense and general Welfare of the United States . . . (Section 8, Article I). Elsewhere in Section 8 we note that the Congress has the power 'to promote the Progress of Science and the Useful Arts'.

There are at least two opposing views of what Congress can or cannot do to promote the general welfare of the people. Thomas Jefferson believed that the laying and collecting of taxes was the *power*, and that the *purpose* was the advancement of the general welfare. He says in a letter:

> They (Congress) are not to lay taxes *ad libitum* for any purpose they please, but only to pay to debts or provide for the welfare of the Union. In like manner, they are not to do anything they please to provide for the general welfare, but only to lay taxes for that purpose.

However, even in the *Federalist Papers* (Ruttand *et al.*, 1977) there

19

is a divergence of opinion over this ambiguous phrase. Hamilton adopted a very broad and liberal meaning. Madison, like Jefferson, believed that the powers of taxation were the main instrument for supporting other powers: that taxation was a means for the government to support itself, not to provide services. However, even from the days of Washington and Jefferson, Congress sided with Hamilton's interpretation and appropriated funds for subsidies for a variety of 'internal improvements'.

The power of Congress to authorise expenditure of public monies for public purposes is not limited by the direct grants of legislative power found in the Constitution.

In 1936 Justice Roberts came down decidedly on the Hamiltonian side, seeing the general welfare clause as conferring a power separate and distinct from those enumerated in Section 8 of Article I, and not restricted exclusively to them.

A curious argument was proposed in President Reagan's 1982 Economic Report concerning the general welfare which had no historical or traditional base in constitutional law or theory. The Administration's use of tax cuts and the reduction of domestic programmes simultaneously would benefit the public, it was argued, by lowering their taxes: 'A general reduction in special interest programs is a necessary step to meet the Constitutional charge to "promote the general Welfare".' Hence, a third argument became executive policy regarding general welfare: the elimination of services.

The phrase 'general welfare' occurs on more than one occasion in the Articles of Confederation. These quotations are worth repeating here, because the phrase is derivative, and has been used almost exclusively to empower Congress to provide legislation on behalf of education.

In Article III of the Articles: 'The said states hereby severally enter into a firm league of friendship with each other, for their common defense, the security of their Liberties, and their mutual and general welfare.' The 'general welfare' here is the common good and welfare of the states, not of its citizens. However, in Article VIII the phrase occurs again: 'All charges of war, and all other expenses [sic] that shall be incurred for the common defense or general welfare, and allowed by the United States in Congress assembled, shall be defrayed out of a common treasury.' Here we have a statement by which the states collectively agree to pay for common incurred expenses, including defence and 'general welfare' items, whatever they might be. The phrase is not limited, as it could appear to be in the Constitution, simply to the *taxing* authority. Did the drafters of these historic documents have in mind that the national government would one day authorise payments on behalf of education and schooling? The 'general welfare' phrase would seem to cover any and all such contingencies. At the end of Article I, Section 8, we find the following statement:

> To make all Laws which shall be necessary and proper for carrying into execution the foregoing powers, and all other powers vested by this Constitution in the Government of the United States, or in any Department or offices thereof.

Clearly, this clause is an expansion, not a limitation of the powers granted to the Congress. Chief Justice John Marshall writing his opinion in *McCulloch vs Maryland* in 1819 noted:

> Let the end be legitimate, let it be within the scope of the Constitution, and all means which are appropriate, which are plainly adapted to that end, which are not prohibited, but consist with the letter and spirit of the Constitution, are constitutional.

Nearly every power, including that of education, has been enlarged under this coefficient or elastic clause.

In each of these constitutional examples — the Tenth Amendment, and Article I, Section 8 — there is no prohibition against the federal government passing laws regarding education. In fact, there are court decisions expressly preventing states from limiting federal authority under the Tenth Amendment.

In the *Federalist Papers*, Madison argued for the 'maximum power the phrase *necessary and proper* will allow'. Garry Wills (1980) comments that Madison believed that the Constitution did not enumerate all the powers that Congress has, nor should the Constitution have enumerated them all. Madison wrote:

> Had the Convention attempted a positive enumeration of the powers necessary and proper for carrying their other powers into effect; the attempt would have involved a complete digest of laws on every subject to which the Constitution relates; accommodated to not only the existing state of things, but to all the possible changes which futurity may produce.

Thus, Madison argued that the Constitution gives the national government *implied* powers not specifically stated. He continued:

Had the Constitution been silent on this head, there can be no doubt that all the particular powers, requisite as means of executing the general powers, would have resulted to the government, by unavoidable implication.

The argument that only the states have an exclusive right to establish and control education and schooling would not have been Madison's belief, nor Hamilton's for that matter. It was definitely not the belief of the Continental Congress. Madison wanted a flexible, an elastic document when he was campaigning for ratification of the Constitution under the pseudonym Publius in the *Federalist Papers*. He intended the Constitution to be functional and realistic, a 'living document', primed to respond to the changing societal and national needs. The federal government was not limited in anything it could do.

2

Education Traditions among Revolutionary Leaders

The worth of the State, in the long run, is the worth of the individuals comprising it.

John Stuart Mill *On Liberty*

The legal documents of the new republic and the democratic ideals that they enshrined set precedents in world history. Yet no mention is made in the Constitution of education: those who framed it were forming a central government, not detailing its legislation. It is in the private and public writings of the illustrious leaders of the revolution that we will find mention of education, and at length. The writings on education of Washington, Jefferson and Madison alone fill a substantial volume. It is my purpose here to sample representative writings of some of the more prominent leaders of the revolutionary and constitutional times to show how widespread and unanimous was their regard for education and its advantages, how necessary for the struggling republic, and how government, even the federal government, ought to assist in that development.

'Education' in the latter half of the seventeenth and early part of the eighteenth centuries meant the process of gaining knowledge. Sometimes it is spoken of as learning, as by Jefferson, and sometimes as schooling. Clearly, it was beyond what we consider simple literacy. Could it be that these men actually contemplated that a federal government, that democratic institution founded to regulate the affairs of the nation, should provide for and sustain education? If the question could be put to them today, I believe they would respond positively in respect of higher education, and perhaps also in respect of elementary and secondary education.

DR BENJAMIN RUSH AND EDUCATION

Benjamin Rush was a delegate from Pennsylvania to the Continental Congress, and a Signatory to the Declaration of Independence and to the Constitution. He was a doctor, and there are those who assert that until the time of the Civil War half the physicians in the country had been trained by him. I have chosen to list a few of his contributions to the furtherance of education to illustrate the thinking prevalent among the leaders of this period in government.

In a letter written in 1786 to Richard Price, a minister and moral philosopher in Britain, Rush proposed a general education plan that gave flexible freedom to students, and encouraged the promotion of more practical learning pursuits, not just the traditional disciplines. Here he may have been under the influence of Benjamin Franklin, who also advocated practical subjects. Rush says in that letter:

> Let our common people be compelled by law to give their children . . . a good English education . . . Let us have colleges in each of the states, and one federal university under the patronage of Congress . . . Let the law of nature and nations, the common law of our country, the different systems of government, history, and everything else connected with the advancement of republican knowledge and principles, be taught by able professors in this university. (Hawkes, 1971)

The idea of a national university run by the federal government will come up repeatedly, supported by Washington, Jefferson and Madison.

There are two points worth noting from this passage. First, that education should be 'compelled by law'. Rush believed that education was too important to be left to the people's discretion — at least the people as he understood that term during his time. Secondly, that there should be a federal university over which Congress would exert control and influence. Federal intervention was not repugnant to Rush, nor was it to others described in this chapter.

A second passage in this same letter requests Richard Price to write a pamphlet on behalf of education for congressional consideration:

> A small pamphlet addressed by you to Congress and the legislature of each of the states, upon this subject [a plan for general education] I am sure would have more weight with our rulers than a hundred publications thrown out by the citizens of this country.

Here is Rush calling upon the respected British philosopher and scholar to lend his reputation and pen to achieve a political end on behalf of education. In fact, what Rush is suggesting, if it were to have been adopted in each of the states, would have been something like a national uniform curriculum. His aim was for Price to influence both the national and state legislatures. There is no indication that Price accepted this bold challenge. Nevertheless, Rush was so indebted to Price that he sent him a lock of Benjamin Franklin's hair after Franklin's death in 1790.

Many of the ideas on education advanced by Rush, especially in his essay 'Of the mode of Education Proper in a Republic', sound today prim and moralistic, as indeed they may have sounded to his contemporaries. For example, he suggests that the ideal student: must be taught to 'amass wealth'; must be 'indulged occasionally in amusements'; must have as his principle pursuits of life, 'study and business'; above all, 'must love life'. These must have been platitudes even then, and they seem oddly inconsistent with Rush's earlier writings on religion and the seriousness he gave to theological pursuits. The Calvinistic, not the Scottish Enlightenment, strains show through this passage. Nevertheless, Rush's prolific writings on education throughout his distinguished medical career, notable for the advancements he made in the care and cure of the mentally disturbed, mark him as both one of education's leading exponents and one who favoured the use of the federal government in its behalf.

It has been suggested that Rush, Jefferson and Noah Webster actually had in mind the use of education as a coercive device for furthering the new form of government: 'Determined to preserve the heritage of the Revolution, to unify the nation, and to inculcate proper principles of government, they advocated a kind of republican indoctrination, hoping that the ensuing enlightenment would bring a salutary uniformity.' (Tyack, 1970)

On the contrary, Rush and Jefferson would have found abhorrent the idea of state domination of education, as opposed to the state furthering the cause of education. I believe that they saw education as a means of making ordinary citizens more knowledgeable about government, particularly republican, democratic government. Education was not then to be the enforcer of democracy but the persuader of its attributes.

A passage in Noah Webster's *Sketches of American Policy*, one of the finest and best-written tracts of this period, demonstrates his concurrence with the views of Rush and Jefferson:

The general education of youth is an Article to which the American states are superior to all nations . . . [Education] is the necessary consequence of the genius of our governments; at the same time, it forms the finest security of our liberties.

The justifiable pride in American schooling is there, but also the fact that education has been a *consequence* of what government has provided. The issue of how government power exerts control over education will surface again in Washington's writings. How could the people who did not participate in or did not know about this new government of centralised power learn about it? The national character of education, its special stamp, would be that its content would be republican government itself. It would be like the job the first Supreme Court justices had when they rode 'circuit' to tell the people what they could and could not do in law.

DR BENJAMIN FRANKLIN AND EDUCATION

Like Thomas Jefferson, Benjamin Franklin did it all, and did it all well. He was printer, author, inventor, diplomat, statesman, acknowledged wit and raconteur, scientist. But in education he is remembered chiefly as the founder of the free public library system, of the academy movement, and of the University of Pennsylvania. Any one of these accomplishments would have singled him out for educational distinction.

His *Poor Richard's Almanack* had unparalleled popularity, and was the first instance in revolutionary America of mass education. His greatest educational contribution was not so much his writings but his gifts as a teacher of men, imparting ideas. His formal writings on education contain mostly exhortations on the development of academies (what we would today consider secondary schools), and in the specification of curricula for academies. A passage in 'Proposals Relating to the Education of Youth in Philadelphia' is significant:

> Almost all Governments have therefore made it the principal object of their Attention, to establish and endow with proper Revenues, such Seminaries of Learning, as might supply the succeeding Age with Men qualified to serve the Public with Honour to themselves, and to their Country.

The theme expressed here is critical: 'governments' should establish schools, and should fund them. There is no distinction here about what kind of government should do this; the implication is that it is one of government's responsibilities.

Like his contemporaries, Franklin was a product of eighteenth century culture and thought. He was captivated, for example, by John Locke's treatise on education (Locke, 1964). But he was much too practical in both thought and action to be circumscribed by ancient modes of learning and teaching. He thought that Latin and Greek should be banned, and he did not want them taught in his Philadelphia academy. He preferred the practical arts and science.

GEORGE WASHINGTON AND EDUCATION

Washington's major contributions to education were a call for a plan for universal education, and in his later years his insistence on a national university. Of the former, he declared:

> The more homogeneous our citizens can be made in these particulars, the greater will be our prospect of permanent union, and a primary object of such a national institution should be the education of our youth in the science of government.
>
> (Eighth Annual Message to Congress 1796)

The homogeneity suggested is the kind of thinking that promotes the more complete *union*, the 'harmony' that was to be characteristic of the new government. Youth needs to know what the government is, and the advantages it has over previous forms of government in America.

It seems natural to find Washington and the others wanting the younger generation, the future leaders, to learn what it was they had created: a new form of government upon the earth, that would allow men to govern themselves more efficiently and wisely, and would include the interests of all the people. Indeed, it would seem strange not to find them arguing for the study of the 'science of government' especially the study of the new American government.

Washington wanted the youth to learn what the government was, and to become more catholic in their thinking:

> For this reason, I have greatly wished to see a plan adopted, by which the arts, sciences, and belles-lettres could be taught in their *fullest* extent, thereby embracing *all* the advantages of European tuition [tradition?], with the means of acquiring the liberal knowledge . . . and, by assembling the youth from the different parts of this rising republic, contributing from their intercourse

27

and interchange of information to the removal of prejudices, which might perhaps arise from local circumstances.

Having so recently conducted a war with Britain, leaders like Washington wanted to train future leaders to know at least what union of the states and federal union meant. He intimated this in a letter to Robert Brooke, then Governor of Virginia in 1795:

> It is with indescribable regret, that I have seen the youth of the United States migrating to foreign countries, in order to acquire the higher branches of erudition, and to obtain a knowledge of the sciences. Although it would be injustice to many to pronounce the certainty of their imbibing maxims not congenial with republicanism, it must nevertheless be admitted that a serious danger is encountered by sending abroad among other political systems those who have not learned the value of their own.

This may seem to smack of paternalism. Learn, youth of America, what your own government is before you experience what other governments are. Rush, Jefferson and Washington are thinking alike: students must learn democracy in education, the 'science of government' as Washington calls it.

What concerned Washington in his declining years was that rival factions and 'jealousies', 'prejudices' would increase and perhaps overcome the Union itself. Could he have conceived the possibility of a civil war in less than a hundred years? He notes in a letter to Hamilton in 1796:

> A century, in the ordinary intercourse, would not have been accomplished what the seven years association in arms did [Hamilton was his aide in the war] but, that ceasing, prejudices are beginning to revive again, and never will be eradicated so effectually by any other means as the intimate intercourse of characters in early life — who, in all probability, will be at the head of their counsels of this country in a more advanced stage of it.

Washington also wanted a plan for universal education: 'The time is therefore come when a plan for universal education ought to be adopted in the United States.' He never proposed what that should be, but, whatever plan he envisaged, it was in keeping with the naturalistic thinking of his day to be a way of diffusing knowledge. The 'diffusion of knowledge' phrase is spread throughout the writings of the eighteenth century thinkers. 'Promote, then, as an object of primary importance, institutions for the general diffusion of knowledge — in proportion as the structure of government gives force to public opinion, it is essential that public opinion should be enlightened', wrote Washington in his farewell address 'To The People of the United States' in 1796. 'Diffusion of knowledge' was the phrase used by James Smithson when he left his legacy to the United States which established the Smithsonian Institution. Jefferson also used the phrase on numerous occasions.

Washington's purpose in wanting to establish a national university was 'to contribute to wear off [sic] those prejudices and unreasonable jealousies, which prevent or weaken friendships and impair harmony of the Union.' (Letter to Thomas Jefferson, 1795)

He also wanted to have the site of the national university in the federal capital so that students could attend the debates in Congress and become acquainted with the principles of a free democracy. 'The Federal City, from its centrality and the advantages . . . ought to be preferred, as a proper site for such a university.'

So strong was this commitment to a national university that he offered a grant towards its endowment. 'I will grant in perpetuity fifty shares in the navigation of Potomac River towards it.' He was willing also to commit these shares (he later offered a hundred of them) to Virginia if that state would found a university. This is now Washington and Lee University. To the roster of founding fathers of universities, we add the name of Washington.

Throughout his writings and proclamations, Washington's thinking on education was a lesson in civic and governmental responsibility. The new form of government was to provide youth and all citizens opportunities to learn about the workings of democracy. Institutions for the diffusion of knowledge, a plan for universal education, a call for the establishment of a national university . . . the ideas, but not the outlines for action, were all there. The details of the operational schemes for all were left to the man to whom we next turn.

THOMAS JEFFERSON AND EDUCATION

Education! Oh Education! The greatest grief of my heart, and the greatest affection of my life! To my mortification I must confess that I have never closely thought, or very deliberately reflected

29

upon the subject which never occurs to me now without producing a deep sigh, a heavy groan, and sometimes tears. *Letter to John Adams, 1814* (in Boyd, 1955)

These are the words of a private not a public man, spoken like a monk rather than a school superintendent, like a scholar who cherishes contemplation and reflection, not a politician. They are certainly not the words of a typical administrator at a school board meeting, or of a professional education representative in testimony in Congress. Yet if the tone sounds touchingly sentimental, uncontemporary, yet somehow humane, it reveals none the less the enormous prestige Jefferson attached to the pursuits of learning.

Equal opportunity for all classes and manners of people was unquestionably Jefferson's hallmark, as legislator, governor, ambassador, president and ex-president. In his personal manner, his administration, and writings he was steadfastly opposed to aristocratic traditions in government or any of its institutions. Jefferson's attempt to establish a systematic plan of general education, reaching all citizens, was never realised. The plan he proposed for Virginia, however, was truly original in scope, indicative of the time he devoted to its conception. It encompassed elementary schooling for up to three years for all children, paid for by all inhabitants according to the general tax rate; colleges for those middle-level years beyond literacy training for those who could afford it; and universities for teaching the sciences. He proposed that students be selected annually from among the poor for further education at public expense. The aristocracy of merit and genius was to be sought after and promoted wherever it existed. These first three bills, for establishing ward schools, district colleges and a university at William and Mary (then chiefly a seminary with legal training) were brought before the Virginia legislature in 1796.

The first bill for the establishment of elementary ward schools was passed but with the politically astute amendment which became its undoing. The amendment contained a provision for local control which left to the county courts the decision of whether or not the bill should be executed. Because the bill's principal effect was to cause the rich to pay for the education of the poor, the bill was never executed in any county. No county was willing to pay for the education of anyone else's children.

The bill to establish a university within the College of William and Mary met a similar fate. The general fear was religious, that the proposed university would be dominated by the Anglicans and for religious purposes. Lesser bills proposed by Jefferson for a library and an art gallery were likewise defeated. In fact, no part of Jefferson's grand scheme for education was ever realised, except his later plan for the University of Virginia. As president he did not abandon his plan for education, but suggested to Congress in his sixth annual message on 2 December 1806 during his second term:

> The present consideration of a national establishment for education, particularly, is rendered proper by [a proposed amendment to the Constitution for new use of public money] that if Congress, approving the proposition, shall yet think it eligible to fund it on a donation of lands, they have it now in their power to endow it with those which will be among the earliest to produce the necessary income. (Boyd, 1955)

And later in the same message:

> Education is here placed among the articles of public care . . . A public institution alone can supply those sciences which, though rarely called for, are yet necessary . . . All the parts of which contribute to the improvement of the country, and some of them to its preservation. (Boyd, 1955)

In his retirement years he wrote a complete educational and curricular system from elementary to professional school with all the subject offerings.

It is ironic, in an age currently developing a competency-based education programme to ensure that students when completing secondary schooling have the minimal skills needed to survive in contemporary society, that Jefferson proposed competency in literacy when he was a young Virginia legislator. Jefferson proposed that no one could become a citizen until he was literate:

> And it is declared and enacted [but it never was] that no person unborn or under the age of twelve years at the time of passing of this act, and who is *compos mentis*, shall, after the age of fifteen years, be a citizen of this commonwealth until he or she can read readily in some tongue, native or acquired.

He had discovered the idea of citizenship based on literacy in the Spanish Constitution, as he describes it in a letter to Mon. Dupont De Nemours in 1816:

In the constitution of Spain . . . there was a principle entirely new to me . . . that no person, born after that day, should even acquire the rights of citizenship until he could read or write . . . Enlighten the people generally, and tyranny and oppressions of body and mind will vanish like evil spirits at the dawn of day . . . the diffusion of knowledge among people is to be the instrument by which it is to be effected. (Boyd, 1955)

Again, that phrase 'diffusion of knowledge' which is so closely associated with our concept of education.

He had an enduring faith in the educated wisdom of the people to maintain the constitutional form of government established by their representatives and in their behalf. He had written to Madison while he was ambassador in Paris in 1787: 'Above all things I hope the education of the common people will be attended to: convinced that on their good sense we may rely with the most security for the preservation of a due degree of liberty.' (Boyd, 1955)

Much later he wrote:

I know no safe depository of the ultimate powers of the society but the people themselves; and if we think them not enlightened enough to exercise their control with a wholesome discretion, the remedy is not to take it from them, but to inform their discretion by education. (Boyd, 1955)

Jefferson's belief in the people as the foundation of a new republic had precedents throughout Western tradition. The history of the course of federal action may have been different in our day had not he forcefully triumphed over the aristocratic thinking. The education of the common person would mean that all citizens would rise to govern themselves in a new nation founded for that purpose.

JAMES MADISON AND EDUCATION

To favour in like manner the advancement of science and the diffusion of information as the best aliment to true liberty.
James Madison, *First Inaugural Address*, 4 March 1809

James Madison profoundly influenced and altered the course of revolutionary America, and shaped the form of government we now take so much for granted. Were it not for the substantive contributions he made to the *Federalist Papers* (ed. Ruttand, 1977), we might not today be able to appreciate his clarity of mind and the scholarly erudition he brought to bear upon American constitutional thought. Yet for all his contributions to constitutional law, he was not a lawyer, as were Jefferson, Hamilton and Monroe. However, this made him no less effective in his ability to persuade and lead his political and constitutional colleagues, who were lawyers, into accepting his definitions and arguments on behalf of congressional legislation, and later, the Constitution.

His writings on education *per se* are not as voluminous as Jefferson's, but his contribution to national government is unparalleled. His views of government are important for our understanding of the relationship between the federal government and education. In 1780 Madison was on record as holding that the Continental Congress possessed powers different from the states and that these powers were implicit in their deliberations. He even wrote a report to the Congress on federal coercion of the states. Madison stood for an implied power of the federal government, even federal coercion of states who refused to obey that power. And he held these beliefs prior to his defence of the Constitution in the *Federalist Papers*. Brant (1965) observes:

All this means that as Madison approached the great task of his life — a leading and guiding part in the writing of the United States' Constitution — he approached as a believer in a strong federal government, in coercion of the states, and in easy discovery of implied powers where none were expressly stated.

This was difficult for some of his colleagues to accept at the time. It would be no less difficult for many leading educators to accept today.

Moreover, Madison even used the war power granted to Congress, expressly delegated to Congress, to prepare legislation which sought 'to put a stop to all commercial intercourse between the inhabitants of the United States of America and the subjects of Great Britain'. Under what authority could Madison, or any legislator, conceive such a scheme? It was certainly not explicit in the Articles: there was no commercial regulation clause. Madison could only have believed that Congress was acting as a separate legal entity through the powers given to it. In any event, his motion passed and was called 'an ordinance relative to the capture and condemnation of prizes'. It was Congress's first ordinance. It has value for our discussion here because it is the first instance in the history of the federal government, preceding constitutional government, of legislation being passed based on powers not specified but implied. I believe it was a giant step for education as well. The theory so often expounded later that the Articles had authority binding only on the states and not on individuals is here given the lie.

Yet Madison had to fight for the doctrine of implied Congressional powers with a timid Congress, at the time waging an inconclusive war along its coast. Brant says:

> The difficulty of maintaining the principle of it, in a government limited to powers expressly delegated and facing jealous and contentious states, aroused him to the danger of the word 'expressly'. Eight years later he omitted it from the Tenth Amendment to the United States Constitution — reserving undelegated powers to the states — and successfully opposed the effort to have it inserted . . . He prevented the cutting down of the United States government to its Confederation level.

Madison's axiomatic belief was that Congress could use monies from the federal treasury, spent on behalf of the 'general welfare', for any purpose defined by Congress. For example, in 1779 the Congress ordered the use of public funds to restore the value of money. The basis for the action was 'the promotion of the general welfare'. Another action Congress took was to educate Indian children at both Princeton and Dartmouth. This is one of the first known examples of spending of federal money for education, based on its jurisdiction under the general welfare clause under the Articles. Thus, the most convincing testimony of the use of federal funds on behalf of education comes from the actual appropriations.

On the eve of the convention to discuss the revision of the Articles from which the Constitution would emerge, Madison made a list of what he felt were abuses in the present form of government and suggested some remedies. He called this document 'Vices of the Political System of the United States'. The content focused almost exclusively on the failure of the state governments to support the federal structure. Here are a few of his 'vices':

● Failure of the states to comply with constitution's requisitions
● Encroachment by the states on federal authority
● Want of concert in matters where common interest requires it
● Want of sanction to the laws, and to the coercion in the government of the confederacy

The list continues, but all in all it is a heavy indictment of the unco-operative states. He who was to become known as 'father of the Constitution' chided the federal system under the Articles for its failure to provide for higher education systems supported by federal funds. It is yet another example which emphatically leads to the conclusion that Madison did not think it unusual to fund national educational institutions from federal funds.

This entire document, completed in April 1787, only one month before the constitutional convention was to begin, emphasised the inability of the states to relate in an organised way with a federal form of government. Even more significantly was Madison's observation that states were passing laws that violated minority and individual rights. His task was to strengthen the national government's power to protect individual and private rights. 'The great desideratum in Government, is such a modification of the Sovereignty as will render it sufficiently neutral between the different interests and factions, to control one part of the Society from invading the rights of another.' The partial outcome of individual violation of rights by the states would become an issue again in less than 100 years after these words were penned, as the Civil War erupted.

Of all the changes Madison contemplated in the new federal system of government none had more depth of purpose than that the federal government should have veto power over the state government's laws: 'Over and above the positive power of regulating trade and sundry other matters in which uniformity is proper, to arm the federal head with a negative *in all cases whatsoever* (italics Madison's) on the local legislatures.' (Letter to Thomas Jefferson, 19 March 1787) 'Let the national Government be armed with a positive and compleat authority in all cases where uniform measures are necessary . . . Let it have a negative in all cases whatsoever on the Legislative Acts of the States.' (Letter to Edmund Randolph, 8 April 1787)

The desired remedies for strengthening central government were firmly shaped in Madison's mind by the spring of that year. He wanted a federal republic strong enough, not just in leadership, but in specified powers, to direct the people's interests, their 'general welfare', and to restrain the diverse interests of the states and check their abridgement of individual rights and liberties. He carried these beliefs with him to Philadelphia to argue his case. He had just finished a long period of study of ancient and world republics at his home in Orange County, Virginia, and had spent seven years in Congress and the Virginia legislature. The building of the Constitution was about to begin and he had adequately prepared himself.

Madison's vision was of a government both *national* and *federal*.

There was to be a supremacy of the national authority, the Union, together with the state authorities subordinate to its powers. When Madison closed his journal for 2 May 1787 with the words 'I left New York for the convention to be held in Philadelphia', the United States were about to enter a new phase of national union and national government. When Madison was 79 years old he wrote to Thomas Gilmes:

> I concur . . . entirely in the expediency of promoting, as much as possible, a sympathy between the interests for public education; and in the particular expedient . . . of providing for a compleat education, at the public expense, of youths . . . whose parents are too poor to defray the cost.

Together with Jefferson, Madison believed in public education at public expense:

> Wherever a youth was ascertained to possess talents meriting an education which his parents could not afford, he should be carried forward at the public expense, from seminary to seminary, to the completion of his studies at the highest. (Letter to W.T. Barry in 1822)

Like other forward-thinking men of his generation, he wanted public education. But, unlike most, he wanted it at public expense. Even his native state of Virginia had turned down such a proposition when Jefferson had submitted legislation for it when he had been a delegate.

Finally, it is his deeds, not just his words, that dignify Madison as a man who promoted education privately. He was appointed to the Board of Visitors for the University of Virginia after its founding in 1817, and upon Jefferson's death, he became its second rector in 1826. He held the post of rector with distinction until 1834, as he had earlier watched the ceremonies conferring the first doctoral degrees in the United States while a student at Princeton. On behalf of the cause of education in general, higher education in particular, and republican government which he believed should support it, he is a man for all seasons, and surely one of our most neglected statesmen, scholars and educators.

The stereotypes we all have of the founders of the republic have sometimes been formed by the romantic and excessively patriotic images from history texts. These stereotypes are misleading, even false. They can prevent us from understanding the view the men themselves held at different times in their lives.

The constitutional doctrine of the formation of the federal government has already been described. Now we see from private and public writing that education was among the highly regarded issues of public care, and that under certain conditions the federal government should take an active part in promoting it. Our prejudices concerning the *existing* role of the federal government in education should not adumbrate the role as it was viewed in the latter part of the eighteenth century by those renowned individuals whose vision shaped the American Republic.

3

Comparing Education in Other National Constitutions

The constitution of any country is the cornerstone of the legal system and is the main referent for future legal thought. Violations against the constitution, however, are not always enforceable by the people. We have seen that the Constitution of the United States does not mention education. But what about the constitutions of other nations, especially those which were formed in the present century? The break-up of colonial empires and the rising tide of independence and nationalism have led to the creation of nations non-existent just a few years ago. The membership of the United Nations is three times as great as it was when it was formed in 1945.

Given the contemporary importance the world attaches to formal education and to literacy, it is not surprising that modern constitutions are more explicit about education than are older constitutions. One helpful method of understanding, then, the relationship between the Constitution of the United States and that of the modern world in education is to study the educational provisions of other constitutions. It is therefore relevant and timely, as a part of our enquiry into constitutional law, federalism and education and government, to compare and analyse the educational statements of a few selected constitutions.

Each of the representative constitutions is unique to its country of origin and deserves more reflective study than is possible here. However, some tentative conclusions are possible even from this brief analysis. The choices are by no means exhaustive or inclusive, although a range of continents and kinds of government are included. I include the constitutions of Malaysia, Canada, Australia and India not only because they have similar parliamentary democracies, but also because they are all former British colonies, as was the United States. I include Russia because of its international influence on world policy even in education, and Indonesia because it is a developing

Asian country like Malaysia. Lastly, I present the United Nations' Declaration on Human Rights to round off the analysis of education within the field of human rights.

A constitutional provision in education may not always be prescriptive in describing all a society expects from its system of education. The constitutional law may be only normative by specifying what tradition or subsequent legislation is to provide for national educational needs, like the extraordinarily short statements found in the Indonesian and Australian constitutions. Both Malaysia and India, however, have written into their constitutions extensive constitutional provisions.

An analysis of constitutional guarantees in the area of human rights, on the other hand, offers fruitful comparison, and demonstrates a nation's concern for individual freedoms and its probable fear of tyrannical government. Issues for comparison from the arena of human rights and protections include: freedom of speech and expression, freedom of assembly, religious freedom, non-discrimination of all forms, the protection of minority rights and freedom of residence and mobility. However, further elements in such a comparative analysis could well be: the right of an individual to an education, the preservation of the national culture, including its native languages, the prominence of the federal power in education and the relationship between the federal authority in education and other legitimate authorities.

THE MALAYSIAN CONSTITUTION AND EDUCATION

A constitution is both the safeguard and guarantee of the powers and authority of a nation. Where, as in England, it is unwritten, it is no less formalised, for Parliament holds all the powers inherent in a constitution and centuries of traditions and legal precedents influence justice and law-making. For nations without such a written history, whose patterns of life dictate new approaches to ordering a new nation, a constitution is necessary to ensure continuity and rational development. Once written, presumably, it becomes the supreme law. 'In Malaysia only the constitution is supreme,' proclaimed Tun Mohamed Suffian, former Lord President of the Federal Court. 'Clearly the legal doctrine that applied in Malaysia is not that Parliament or any other body is supreme but that the constitution is supreme,'

Is not the Malaysian legislature also supreme because in almost all instances it has the power to amend the constitution? Are not the courts supreme because they can declare unconstitutional a federal law? Parliaments are not supreme because, although they are able

39

to add new legal entries and therefore meanings to the constitution, they may not violate its essential meanings, which generally the courts are left to interpret. Suffian says in this regard: 'Thus Parliament may legislate only specific subjects, such as . . . education . . . In this field where it enjoys legislative competence, it is supreme in the sense that there is no law which it cannot make, repeal or amend.' Neither is Parliament in Malaysia supreme in its relation to the states, as Suffian (1975) again explains:

> Outside federal (and concurrent) subjects Parliament is not supreme, and if it makes a law on, say, local government or Muslim law outside the Federal Territory, both being state subjects, that law may be declared void by the courts.

A nation's constitution will therefore reflect the important characteristics of education within a framework of other governmental provisions and services; it will also reflect how a nation regards fundamental human freedoms. The contributions in the constitution of Malaysia to education are lengthy and more fully documented than in nearly any other constitution. The specific educational provisions can be grouped as follows:

- a non-discrimination clause
- a federal financial provision for education in any educational institution
- a guarantee of religious groups to establish and maintain schools
- a clause outlining the federal authority in education
- the preferential treatment of Muslims in education

Educational non-discrimination

The Malaysian Constitution prohibits discrimination in education, 'on the grounds of religion, race, descent, or place of birth'. The clause expressly prohibits discrimination in administration, admission procedures and fees payment. Another clause allows the possibility for any religious group to establish and maintain schools and to provide instruction in its own religion. The same article allows for federal or state law to provide special financial aid for Muslim institutions or instruction in the religion of Islam.

Federal financial provision

The Constitution further prohibits discrimination in the disbursement of funds from any public authority either for financial aid to any institution or to students. In the country's past history there has been discrimination in the disbursement of public monies whereby individuals in places of financial power use their influence to favour one class or ethnic group over another. The constitution seeks to prohibit this practice.

Religious freedom

Article 12 states:

> Every religious group has the right to establish and maintain institutions for the education of children and provide therein instruction in its own religion, and there shall be no discrimination on the ground only of religion in any law relating to such institutions or in the administration of any such law; but federal or state law may provide for special financial aid for the establishment or maintenance of Muslim institutions or instruction in the Muslim religion or persons professing that religion.

There are two aspects worth noting in this Article. First, freedom of religious education is guaranteed constitutionally. Indeed, in many ways it could not have been otherwise, since there have always been in peninsular Malaysia schools which catered separately for the Chinese, Malay, Hindu, and, later, Christian populations.

The reason for the separatism in the school, which still tends to create problems for educationists in Malaysia today, is that the British at the time of the colonial administration found it convenient to keep the schools of the different ethnic groups distinct. At the time it seemed advantageous to keep schools for Chinese, since they principally worked in the tin mines, separate from schools for the Hindus, since they worked on the rubber plantations — if indeed the Indians were provided schools by their plantation employers at all. For the Malays, the British were content to provide elitist schools for the sons of the chiefs and rajas, in which the language medium was, understandably, English. The advantages associated with providing English-speaking schools to an entire colonial administration were advanced on several occasions by some of the more astute English administrators and

41

school inspectors. However, they were just as soon dismissed by the authorities as impractical, expensive or unnecessary to the British mission.

The second aspect worth noting about this constitutional Article is that the Muslim religion in all matters educational will receive special government consideration and aid.

Federal authority

Article 93 permits the federal government to conduct inquiries, surveys and to gather information as seems appropriate. It also directs the state governments to render assistance to the federal government as it executes any activity under this article. Article 94 extends the conduct of research and experimentation in education, and further extends the federal authority to the giving of advice and technical assistance to state governments.

The federal list is a categorisation of subjects over which the federation has federal executive and legislative authority. The list for education is somewhat extensive and specific, and I cite it here in full:

13. Education, including:
    (a) elementary, secondary and university education; vocational and technical education; training of teachers; registration and control of teachers, managers and schools; preparation of special studies and research; scientific and literary societies; and
    (b) Libraries; museums; ancient and historical monuments and records; archaeological sites and remains.

One might think it odd to have the authority for the process of education categorised with such functions as responsibility for the burial sites of ancestors and literary societies. Yet it is precisely because education in Malaysia is viewed as a continuous thread leading from the past to the present that it is included. Education, as encapsulated in the federal authority, is a direct link with the history of the nation and all its traditions. Consequently, it is most appropriately included with all that which preserves that heritage.

Elsewhere, in Article 132, education is defined as one of the public services, along with the police, armed services and railways. Like these other governmental services, the constitution also provides for a Commission, in this case the Education Service Commission, composed of a chairman and four members appointed by the king, whose collective responsibility it is to determine matters relating to the appointment, promotion and discipline of federal education officials. When teachers became government servants Article 141a was added to the Constitution in 1973 establishing an Education Service Commission.

Thus, the constitution provides that Parliament can make any law with respect to those subjects which the federal and state authorities deal with jointly. State law cannot, obviously, make any law that affects citizens outside the state boundaries. If any state law is inconsistent with federal law, the federal law will prevail and the state law will be void.

Preference for muslims

Article 153 gives to the king and chief executive (the Yang Di Pertuan Agong), the authority to increase the number of Malaysian students in any educational institution and to reserve a number of places for Malays (and natives of Borneo states) as he may deem fit. The educational quota system permitted by the constitution is part of a large quota system guaranteed by the constitution in all kinds of governmental services, particularly the licensing and issuing of permits for legitimate interests. The intent is 'to safeguard the special position of the Malays' and to insure that there are enough places for them in government, business and education. Specifically mentioned are educational and training privileges, special facilities, and the operation of trades and businesses.

CANADA, CONSTITUTION AND EDUCATION

The political problems of the supremacy of the central government over state governments, of the guarantee of individual rights and the relationship of the individual to respective government have not been completely resolved in all democracies. Consider the case of Canada.

Canada has officially operated under the authority of the British North America Act of 1867, an embarrassment and an inconvenience to the Government of Canada because it meant that amendments, prior to the Constitution Act of 1981, had to be passed by the British Parliament in Westminster. The Constitution Act of 1981 does not spell

43

out in detail the roles and functions of governments; instead, it defines the liberties and freedoms of individuals and guarantees them.

The strain between federal and provincial governments was never more evident than in the attempt by Quebec in 1980 to secede from the confederation. Other provincial governments strengthened their hands by passing their own legislation empowering them to limit their federal participation and increase their responsibilities in such areas as natural resources exploration and development, fishing rights, taxing authority, French and English language priorities, and the rights of the aboriginal natives.

This provincial emphasis over the federal rights to decide certain issues is reminiscent of the American struggle over constitutional adoption and ratification. But the power of the central government to control the destiny of the union, after Quebec's referendum failed in 1980 to negotiate a separate sovereignty association, was *the* dominant issue. This intense debate illuminated the lack of clear and demarcated powers between the state and provincial governments and their relationship to central authority. Contributing to that core question were the twin problems of different languages, both claiming superiority, and the role of the citizen in choosing a future government.

In many ways, the debate over the new Constitution for Canada read like the scenario for the American dilemma in the late 1780s. Provincial governments were proclaiming sovereignty over off-shore resources, fishing rights and communications. They had erected barriers to free trade and free movement of goods. Provincial governments were chafing over federal requests for increased sharing of provincial wealth. The issue was not between England and Canada but within Canada.

The new Canadian Constitution of 1981 goes much farther than the United States' Constitution in its charter of freedoms and rights. It not only includes all the first amendment rights but adds specific voting rights, mobility rights, legal rights and rights of equality and language preference. The specific education section reads: 'Nothing in this Charter abrogates or derogates from any rights or privileges guaranteed by or under the Constitution of Canada in respect of denominational, separate or dissentient schools.' On the face of it, this passage seems strange. But it guarantees the continuing force of the British North America Act, which prohibits the making of any law which infringes the rights of the different denominational schools. The entire section of the British North America Act is worth quoting here.

93. In and for each Province the Legislature may exclusively make Laws in relation to education, subject to the following Provisions:
    (1) Nothing in any such law shall prejudicially affect any Right or Privilege with respect to Denominational Schools which any class of Persons have by Law in the Province of the Union;
    (2) All the Powers, Privileges, Duties at the Union by Law conferred and imposed in Upper Canada on the Separate Schools and School Trustees of the Queen's Roman Catholic Subjects shall be and the same extended to the Dissentient Schools of the Queen's Protestant and Roman Catholic Subjects in Quebec.
    (3) Where in any Province a System of Separate or Dissentient Schools exists by Law at the Union or is thereafter established by the Legislature of the Province, an appeal shall lie to the Governor General in Council from any Act or Decision of any Provincial Authority affecting any rights or Privilege of the Protestant or Roman Catholic Minority of the Queen's subjects in relation to education.

The language is legalistic, strained and overdone, but the law clearly seeks to protect the rights of minority and religious schools, Catholic or Protestant, in those geographic locales where one or the other is a minority.

Prior to the Constitution Act of 1981, the Canadian Constitution lacked a clear definition of human liberties, akin to the American Constitution lacking a Bill of Rights. The new Constitution leaves intact the schooling question by preserving the religious independence of the schools. This is perhaps a unique contribution to world constitutional theory and government.

AUSTRALIAN CONSTITUTION AND EDUCATION

The Australian Constitution offers the possibility of studying the supreme rule of law of a country which is both a former British colony and a federation of states. Early in Australia's brief history came the need, as with Malaysia and the United States, to weld the allegiances of the separate states more closely into a federation bound by written constitution. This federation was to be a union of distinctive colonies, with a federal executive and legislature and a common constitutional agreement. Its constitutional features that afford comparison in education include:

- the relationship of the federal to the state governments
- the relationship of the individual to the government
- and the special educational provision

The Australian Constitution makes no provision for regulating or defining the powers of the individual states. Sawer (1975) elaborates:

> The states derive their constitutions and powers from British statutes, just as much as the Australian Government derives its structure and powers from the British statute embodying the Constitution: it follows that the federal set is inconsistent with the state set.

The main force of the federal constitution was neither to resolve between authorities, nor to establish a centralised government that exceeded the jurisdiction of the states in all matters. Common defence, taxation and the like — as well as independence — have usually been the motivating force behind a federal constitution.

The founding fathers of the Australian Constitution, not wishing to dominate the affairs of the individual states by usurping their legislative or executive authority, did not rectify the relation of the states to the parent government in England. As late as 1974, the states, according to Sawer,

> were still subject to Colonial Laws of Validity Act of 1865, and unable to amend or repeat British legislation applicable to them, and their powers of extra-territorial legislation were limited. They remained formally in a semi-colonial condition out of step with the development of Australia as a whole.

The concept of the sovereignty of the people was not a consideration of the writers of the federal constitution, though it does exist in some state constitutions.

> The Australian federal system is not like that of the U.S.A., based squarely on a constitutional theory of sovereignty vested in the people, and . . . a small component of popular sovereignty has crept into some state constitutions. (Sawer, 1975)

The federal constitution does not extend the full range of liberties to the individual that other constitutions do, principally because popular sovereignty was not the theory behind its construction. The most striking example is the guarantee of religious tolerance. However, it binds only the Commonwealth and not the corresponding states:

116. The Commonwealth shall not make any law for establishing any religions, or for imposing any religious observance, or for prohibiting the free exercise of any religion, and no religious test shall be required as a qualification for any office, or any public trust under the Commonwealth.

Another section prohibits discrimination, but only when a citizen is in another state. Unbelievably, it does not prohibit discrimination within one's own state.

117. A subject of the Queen, resident in any state, shall not be subject in any other state to any disability or discrimination which would not be equally applicable to him if he were a subject of the Queen resident in such other state.

Included in the powers of Parliament, the equivalent of the federal list, and buried deep in an enumeration of those specific federal responsibilities, lies the only phrase that pertains to education. It is included in one of the five adopted amendments and reads:

51. The Parliament shall, subject to this Constitution, have power to make laws for the peace, order, and good government of the Commonwealth with respect to . . . the provision of maternity allowance, widows' pensions, child endowment, unemployment, pharmaceutical, sickness and hospital benefits, medical and dental services [and] benefits to students and family allowance.

It is worthwhile noting that the provision is an individual and not an institutional benefit: the direct beneficiary is a student, not a school. Adopted in 1946, the year following the cessation of World War II hostilities in the Pacific theatre, in which Australia suffered severely, a strong social service and welfare provisions and constitutional amendment such as this is to be expected.

INDIA AND EDUCATION

As a South Asian country whose developmental problems, economic as well as educational, both mirror and magnify those of its Asian neighbours, India is a prime example of how constitutional law-makers regard education. The principal element in the Indian Constitution relating to education include fundamental rights, the recognised freedoms, the preservation of language and culture, minority rights and the relative jurisdiction between local, state and federal responsibilities in education.

The ringing, eloquent words of the preamble set the tone for the litany of legal provisions which follow:

> We the people of India, having solemnly resolved to constitute India into a sovereign, democratic republic and to secure to all its citizens: Justice, social, economic and political; Liberty of thought, expression, belief, faith and worship; Equality, of status and opportunity; and to promote among them all Fraternity, assuring the dignity of the individual and the unity of the Nation in our constituent assembly this twenty-sixth day of November, 1949, do hereby adopt, enact, and give ourselves this constitution.

The Indian Constitution secures the pre-eminence of the constitution in establishing fundamental rights by prohibiting the state from making any law which attempts to diminish or abrogate them:

> The State shall not make any law which takes away or abridges the rights conferred by this part (Fundamental Rights) and any law made in contravention of this clause shall, to the extent of the contravention, be void.

Shortly after, there follows the non-discrimination clause: 'The State shall not discriminate against any citizen on grounds only of religion, race, caste, sex, place of birth or any of them.' Later clauses prohibit employment and appointment discrimination. The fundamental rights are clearly and unequivocally stated:

> All citizens shall have the right . . . (a) to freedom of speech and expression; (b) to assemble peaceably and without arms; (c) to form associations or unions: (d) to move freely throughout the territory of India: (e) to reside and settle in any part of the Territory of India: (f) to acquire, hold and dispose of property; and (g) to practise any profession, or to carry on any occupation, trade or business.

Missing from the list of fundamental rights is the right to an education, although later sections outline government responsibilities.

The freedom of religious expression is paramount, and several sections of the constitution repeat its importance. A qualifier in the clause does not detract from the force of the provision: 'Subject to public order, morality and health . . . all persons are equally entitled to freedom of conscience, and the right freely to profess, practise and propagate religion.' In many respects, this constitutional provision goes further than most constitutions in allowing not only for religious profession and practice, but also for propagation and proselytising. Other sections discussing language, or admission to an educational institution, or the rights of minorities, also prohibit religious discrimination. For example: 'No children shall be denied admission into any educational institution maintained by the State or receiving aid out of State funds on grounds only of religion, race, caste, language or any of them.' Further, minorities are protected not only in their practice of religion but in establishing educational institutions for their children; and the state is prohibited from interfering in the administration of such institutions: 'The State shall not, in granting aid to educational institutions, discriminate against any educational institution on the ground that it is under the management of a minority whether based on religion or language.'

What are the federal government's responsibilities towards education in India? For all practical purposes they are limited to higher education, and specific scientific and technical education programmes. One provision in particular imparts to the government sweeping powers to regulate and standardise curriculum, admission, quality-control measures, teachers and teaching practices: '66. Co-ordination and determination of standards in institutions for higher education or research and scientific and technical institutions.'

By contrast, the only concurrent educational provision is 'vocational and technical training of labour'. The District Council, the political body formed from a regional jurisdiction, does have constitutionally the power to 'establish, construct or manage primary schools'. The District Council is even granted the power to 'prescribe the language and the manner in which primary education shall be imparted in the primary schools in the district'.

In sum, the Constitution of India provides for religious, ethnic (language), minority, and fundamental freedoms for all its people, and grants to the federal government authority over higher education, while giving to local districts control over primary or elementary education.

RUSSIA AND EDUCATION

The Constitution of the Union of Soviet Socialist Republics dates from the end of 1934, after the Soviet Communist Party had succeeded in consolidating its power base within the country under the reign of Josef Stalin. The Soviet Federal Constitution gives the federal government exceptionally wide powers in all phases of administration. In education, the Soviet Constitution provides for 'basic principles' to be maintained throughout all the republics of the Union. It also makes provision to ensure that the constitutions of the member republics conform to the federal constitution.

Some unique features of the Soviet Constitution extend to the separate republics. One is that a constituent republic has the constitutional power to secede from the federation — a provision unheard of in any other constitution. A second feature is that each republic can by itself enter into foreign relations and reach agreements with other countries.

The Constitution not only gives fundamental rights to all citizens, it also imposes certain duties and responsibilities on them. Article 121 of the Constitution details their educational rights. First, the Soviet Constitution ensures universal, free, compulsory education. It provides state stipends and scholarship aid for students who excel in their studies, or in selected areas where there is a shortage of personnel or trained workers — teachers of handicapped children for example. Citizens also receive instruction in their native language, and free vocational, agricultural and machine and technical training on state farms or factories or their places of work. As a result of this heavy thrust in education, Russia has nearly attained a zero figure in illiteracy. In 1913 barely one quarter of the population was literate. The overcoming of Russian illiteracy has been a staggering achievement in human development. The extensiveness of the higher educational training facilities and programme is remarkable. A constitutional amendment in 1947 allowed the state to charge a small fee for the relief of the expense of higher education. Generally, it is not more than 10 per cent of a worker's salary.

The position of women in general, but particularly in education, is relevant here. Article 122 of the Soviet Constitution grants equal rights to women in all spheres of life — work, leisure, pay and education. As a result, the achievements of women throughout Soviet life have set a pattern of sexual non-discrimination. Women not only hold many highly esteemed positions but account for nearly half of the labour force and command their share of coveted positions in medicine, education and the life-sciences.

INDONESIA AND EDUCATION

The Constitution of the Republic of Indonesia is remarkably spare and lean in its legal description. Associated closely, however, with the constitutional provision in education is the preservation of the cultural heritage. The chapter on education is as follows:

> Chapter XIII. Article 31. (1) Every citizen shall have the right to obtain an education. (2) The Government shall establish and conduct a national educational system which shall be regulated by statute.
> Article 32. The Government shall advance the national culture of Indonesia.

In provisions which are specific to education the Indonesian Constitution is silent as to detail. Whatever requirements are deemed necessary for the operation and maintenance of the education system, receive their impetus from law or statute from the ruling assembly.

In making a comparison between the Indonesian Constitution and that of others, it is worthwhile noting some of its other special features which cover the broad area of religious freedom and social rights. First, the Indonesian Constitution designates a specific religious principle — belief in God — and guarantees religious freedom to every resident:

> Chapter XI Religion. Article 29. (1) The State shall be based upon Belief in One, Supreme God. (2) The State shall guarantee freedom to every resident to adhere to his respective religion and to perform his religious duties in conformity with that religion and that faith.

Thus, Indonesia's Constitution ensures religious freedom by means of that highest law.

Secondly, the constitution specifically seeks to ensure the preservation and continuity of the island republic's culture and traditions. The educational and historical traditions are closely intertwined. A particularly significant phrase is that the culture will be enriched by absorbing foreign cultures:

Chapter XIII. Education Article 31, clause 2. The ancient and indigenous cultures which are to be found as cultural heights in all the regions throughout Indonesia are part of the nation's culture. Cultural efforts should lead towards advance in civilisation, culture and unity, without rejecting from foreign cultures new materials which can bring about the development of or enrich the nation's own culture, as well as raise the height of the Indonesian nation.

That last passage about the assimilation of other cultures into that of its own is a singularly unique constitutional phenomenon.

Thirdly, the Indonesian Constitution provides for the use of many languages:

In the areas processing languages of their own which are actively used by the people concerned (for instance, Javanese, Sudanese, Maduese and so forth) those languages will be respected and also cared by the State. Those languages are a part of the living culture of Indonesia.

Because language is considered a part of culture, the constitution protects the users of living languages, with obvious impact on the schools in order to preserve the medium of communication of a part of the culture.

Fourthly and last, is freedom of expression. The Indonesian Constitution says that 'Freedoms of association and assembly, of expressing thoughts and of issuing writing and the like shall be prescribed by statute.' Thus, these freedoms are not guaranteed by constitutional law but by the national legislative law. (Chapter X, Article 28)

With 37 Articles, most only one sentence long, in only nine pages with a few pages of commentary, the Indonesian Constitution is amazingly compact and terse. Much of its powers are referred to the legal-making body to resolve as is necessary.

A nation's constitution may be brief, as in Indonesia's, or lengthy, as in India's or Malaysia's, but it is none the less the ultimate determinant of a nation's future development. It sums up much of what a nation represents to itself and to the world community. It is a document which places for all the world to see its plan for rational governance of its internal affairs and its organisation for human services.

INTERNATIONAL EDUCATION RIGHTS: THE UNITED NATIONS' DECLARATION

Instantaneous communication by satellite and international air travel have shortened the distances and abbreviated the time for the people of one nation to know those of others. Is it not possible, then, for an international rationale and agreement to emerge among nations on those principles essential for world survival and peace, the development of a better social order and humane practices of governments towards its peoples? A document to this end does in fact exist. A proclamation of the United Nations, it too can illuminate our inquiry into the relationship of law and educational development by putting into clearer focus international agreements on human rights.

The Universal Declaration of Human Rights was adopted and proclaimed by the United Nations General Assembly in 1948. That historic assembly called upon member delegates and nations: 'to cause it to be disseminated, displayed, read and expounded, principally in schools and other educational institutions, without distinction based on political states of countries or territories'. The Universal Declaration embodies all the fundamental human rights collectively discussed and resolved by member states with fresh memories of the convulsive events of World War II. Whether or not its universal adoption by the nations has so entered the minds of their citizens as to prevent World War III remains to be witnessed. Wars begin in the minds of men, and it is the minds of men which must first be converted to the concepts of peace.

Article 26 on education is especially appropriate because it embodies those basic rights that free men and women everywhere would like to see as their nation's contribution to human advancement and opportunity:

(1) Everyone has the right to education. Education shall be free, at least in the elementary and fundamental stages. Elementary education shall be compulsory. Technical and profession education shall be made generally available and higher education shall be equally accessible to all on the basis of merit.

(2) Education shall be directed to the full development of the human personality and to the strengthening of respect for human rights and fundamental freedoms. It shall promote understanding, tolerance and friendship among all nations, racial or religious groups, and shall further the activities of the United Nations for maintenance of peace.

(3) Parents have a prior right to choose the kind of education that shall be given to their children.

We can all nod in agreement with these fundamental educational principles so nobly expressed, yet we can also name countries in which today these universally accepted principles are not in fact practised. This gives cause enough for educators and enlightened citizens everywhere to make known their just concerns. Political repression, unjust usurpation of basic human rights, denial of privileges and autocratic rule are rampant in many areas of the world.

It is equally necessary to strengthen those democratic nations and their institutions which practise universal suffrage and, in so doing, ideologically oppose institutions which suppress fundamental human rights. It is not utopian to will that men and women be universally entitled to a civilised life and to receive respect as persons and freedom to define their lives. To realise the importance of human rights we have only to consider what happens when we deny them fulfilment. The stage is then set for collective unrest which leads to repression, strife and war.

The right to education and the opportunities it brings come within the category of social and cultural rights that, in addition to political and civil rights, are necessary for effective participation in the life of the nation. The various covenants or treaties ratified by the United Nations cover a mosaic of problems that derive from the denial of these rights and which have led to genocide, racial discrimination, enforced migration and expatriation, slavery, the lack of rights for women, denial of the right of access to information and many other evils. In a world where half the children reach maturity without any education, often because there are no schools available, where 40 per cent of adults cannot read or write, then the right to education can be seen as overriding. The target proposed by the United Nations Educational, Scientific and Cultural Organisation (UNESCO) is not too ambitious: by the end of this millennium to eliminate illiteracy and to ensure for every child at least six years of primary education. Education is not limited to the rudiments of literacy. The UN Declaration also sets out to establish principles which guide young people into responsible adulthood by educating all their faculties, thus to pledge themselves to the goals of peace, liberty and human dignity.

The problem of protecting human rights, in education as well as in civil affairs, is a matter for governments as well as for individuals. There can be no freedoms where men and women are not aware of their rights. There can be no enjoyment of human pursuits when a man cannot feed his family. A person cannot be free if the nation of which he is a member does not allow him the right to voice his opinions. The exercise of human rights and governments' protection of them demand daily vigilance by the peoples of the world. The Constitution of Malaysia goes farther than most constitutions in enunciating human rights and in providing for firm educational principles. The United Nations Declaration, its context moral and non-political, goes beyond any legal definition.

In the final analysis, education mirrors the social development of nations because it is at the heart of what people consider their most important and delicate responsibility: the education of their children and young people. Educational policy does not exist in a societal vacuum, but thrives in a cultural context founded in freedom and based in law. Educational policy will never consciously contradict the law, though it may seek to change it, nor publicly flout it; but educational practice is not always in keeping with the law. Although the constitution, the legislature and various statutes may prescribe what can and cannot be done or omitted, none of us is so naïve as to believe that what is written is universally believed or practised. Law is based on the deliberations of rational people. Were the consequences of their deliberations adhered to, there would be no need of an elaborate system of judicial administration.

The chief educational goal for any country is the promotion in the minds of the young of an awareness of the value of human freedoms and liberties. The world's peace depends upon it. Educators, then, will not only be knowledgeable about their rights and freedoms, but have the determination to foster greater knowledge of them among the young and uninformed. Comparing and analysing written constitutions is obviously not the only method of delineating how a nation's legal basis influences education. It is only the first step of a longer journey, unfortunately beyond the scope of this inquiry. Educational practice builds upon what a constitution guarantees. High-sounding constitutional phrases read well, but we are all aware that social injustice and abrogation of human freedoms exist in the world, even among countries dedicated to platforms of high human advancement.

Part Two: The Federal Judiciary and Education

The judicial power of the United States shall be vested in one Supreme Court . . . The judicial power shall extend to all cases, in law and equity, arising under this Constitution.

Article III, *US Constitution*

America, America!
God mend thy every flaw
Confirm thy soul
In self control
Thy liberty in law.

America The Beautiful

4

Education and the Federal Judiciary

IN DEFENCE OF FREEDOMS

The Constitution established itself as the final criterion upon which all other laws would be judged. It is not merely a formality that federal officials take an oath upon assuming office to protect and defend the Constitution. No state nor any individual acting on behalf of a state can lawfully usurp that prerogative that is the Supreme Court's special power. There is of course a lengthy history of the denial of rights and infringements on constitutional freedoms — from the Alien and Sedition Acts, the martial law that prevailed during the Civil War, to the odious era of Reconstruction, McCarthyism, Watergate — that should make us uncomfortable of our past.

Both states and schools have, as this history reveals, ignored and denied guaranteed freedoms. Certainly, the federal government has been a party to allowing and creating abuses which are a blotch in our history. Either from ignorance or malice, freedoms allowed to erode for the few can be lost for the many. The preservation and extension of those freedoms which we all enjoy requires the sternest schooling in vigilance. It is evasion of civic responsibility, not subjugation by force, that is the greatest danger in a democracy.

Unless the people in a democracy express their preferences and fight for their rights, each generation's sense of liberty will be gradually eroded. Those who passively observe injustice done to the few must alarm the many. As Solon observed about the proposed plan for Athenian democracy in the sixth century BC: 'We can have justice whenever those most injured by injustice are as outraged as those who have least been.' Are those who are most alive to the presumed dangers of federal government actually prepared to return to smaller forms of government? Are local governments the most effective instruments for the preservation of individual liberties? The history of the United States indicates that they are not. The prevalent assumption is that there is a descending scale of freedom from federal to local government, and an ascending scale of inefficiency from local to federal. This concept has no foundation in American history or experience, even though it appears to be the conventional wisdom. Somehow in education the myth prevails that only local citizens can come to grips with the national problems that face the educational system. It is the predominant reasoning in education and, although traditional in the hearts of the citizens, actually has no constitutional base. The deep distrust of rule by the majority probably stems from a fear that something we cherish will somehow be taken from us.

This paradox of majority rule and the preservation of special interests remains with us in the debate over the extent of federal control in the schools. When we witness the deprivation of rights of an individual, a class or a social or racial group, we either ignore it or delude ourselves into thinking we have a special case on our hands. We seem not embarrassed by this inconsistency and instead believe that we have been especially singled out by the federal government to obey its injunction. When we absolutely cannot rationalise what the balance of the educational relationship should be between federal, state and local educational programmes, we allow the courts to decide for us. The judiciary has become by default the church of good conduct and the decisions it is being asked to make are the decisions the schools have not made. Individual and collective uncertainty and indecisiveness in education reveal the deep ambiguity of schools to adjust to the patterns of social and educational quality.

The court's job of balancing the educational scale of justice almost always involves balancing the right of the state to exist and administer institutions for the public good, with the right of the individual not to be discriminated against by a state institution. Schools have a right to regulate activities according to the laws of the state and, for example, to compel attendance. So students may be forbidden to wear armbands protesting against an unjust war; or petition for redress of financial inequality in school funding; or petition for damages against the school for not instructing in basic literacy; or seek admission having been denied because of race, sex or an arbitrary quota. Student ideas may be dangerous, the language abusive, the mannerisms and eccentricities offensive, but there has to be sympathetic indulgence over their educational, constitutional entitlements. It is this seeming permissiveness that irritates in a democracy, this protection of social and political pariahs who test the Constitution's limits and people's patience.

Against the claims of the state to regulate as it sees fit the actions of its educational institutional life, must be weighed those fundamental and traditional rights which confront our active historical consciousness.

THE SUPREME COURT

An obvious weakness in the Articles of Confederation had been the omission of a judiciary. Prior to the constitutionally created Supreme Court, states were not bound by the legal actions of other states, and citizens could ignore the legalities of one state by moving to another. The state's power was supreme and there were no guarantees of individual freedoms. The constitutional architects sought to remedy that deficiency with a federal judiciary no less powerful than the executive and legislative.

The court may hear cases, but it does not initiate them. It specifies what the law is when it decides lawsuits, and this extends to all kinds of statutes, treaties and regulations. All other branches of government must defer to the court's views, even though state courts often share jurisdiction.

Most education matters have found their way to the Supreme Court through the state courts by way of appeal. An individual's case may be heard by the court only if the court wishes to hear it. One form of review is *certiorari*, the Latin for 'to be made more precise, definite or certain'. The higher court requests the lower court to turn over the case to it. A litigant may petition the court to hear the case, but the court has the discretion to decide whether or not it will. Cases may reach the court, however, on appeal — as a matter of right — or by certification where possible errors of law may have been committed.

Certiorari is one of the most frequent writs used by the Supreme Court to hear cases. More often than not the writ is denied, usually because the four justices required to review the case cannot agree among themselves on the merits for judging the case. This does not necessarily imply agreement with the lower court's decision. Ninety-five per cent of cases brought before the court are thus rejected for want of an agreement for a hearing.

The constitutional basis for judicial review was first tested in 1803 under Chief Justice John Marshall when the court ruled that an Act of Congress was unconstitutional. Late on his last night in presidential office, John Adams had signed the commission of a man called Marbury to be Justice of the Peace for the District of Columbia. Thomas Jefferson, the new President, had commanded his Secretary of State, James Madison, not to deliver the commission papers. Marbury appealed directly to the Supreme Court citing the Judiciary Act as his legal basis. Chief Justice Marshall believed that Marbury was entitled to his commisson, but found the Judiciary Act unconstitutional in giving the court powers not conveyed in the Constitution. The court found that the Congress had over-stepped its authority by passing an act expanding the court's power. It was hence null and void.

This decision established the Constitution as the firm basis for all laws, and created the court as the supreme arbiter in deciding constitutional issues, national or state. The principle of judicial review has not been challenged since. Although Congress may indeed limit the court's jurisdiction, it cannot enlarge or reduce the court's constitutional powers except by constitutional amendment.

Even with the expanded role of the courts in education, the judiciary is perhaps the least understood of all government branches. Yet it is to the courts that individuals and institutions turn when seeking petition for rights and freedoms and against abuse. It is safe to say that no issue, once solved solely by the school authorities, has been exempt from adjudication in the courts. Religion in the schools, the relationship between local boards and state boards, school finance, school property, personnel administration, teacher organisations, individual pupils, as well as racial segregation, all have precedents in court cases. Most major educational issues eventually become judicial.

None has been so obvious to the public as that of school segregation. It may even be regrettable that such an important social issue had eventually to be settled by the Supreme Court; but Congress had not acted, there was no apparent leadership from the executive and the schools themselves clearly had not instituted appropriate relief.

Segregation itself took many forms: sex, religion, social class, wealth and ethnicity. No greater conflict existed in the schools than segregation by race or ethnicity, particularly of blacks. It was pervasive, entrenched and seemingly impervious to change. When the change came it was not initially abrupt and tumultuous, but the judicial reasoning of this educational issue which had found its way into the courts was consistently against the prevailing educational trend.

Segregation resulted partly from the inability of the Constitution to define citizenship, The celebrated *Dred Scott* case did not help. Until the Fourteenth Amendment, the general onus of defining citizenship fell upon the several states. Slaves could not become citizens under any existing federal or state law.

The Missouri Compromise of 1820 admitted Maine, carved out of Massachusetts, into the Union as a free state, while permitting Missouri the right to establish slavery. Congress had to repeal the Act in the mid-1850s because of antagonism in Nebraska and Kansas, where slavery would otherwise also have been permitted. Nebraska wanted no slavery. The Act read in part: 'All questions pertaining to slavery in the territories and in the new states therefrom are to be left to the people residing therein, through their appropriate representatives.' Even before the *Dred Scott* decision, therefore, the national government had not determined national citizenship as anything other than derived from state citizenship. One could not be a citizen of the United States without first being a citizen of a state.

Dred Scott was black. Born in Virginia, he had been taken by his owner, an army medical officer, to Missouri, then to Illinois and Minnesota. Illinois and Minnesota were then free, although Minnesota was still a territory. In 1838 he was taken back to Missouri where his owner died. He brought suit against his owner's widow who tried to claim him, on the grounds that his residence in Illinois and Minnesota no longer made him subject to slavery. Chief Justice Taney concluded that a slave does not become free when his owner takes him to reside in a free state or territory. Although viewed from the perspective of history the decision cast a pall over the rights of non-whites, specifically blacks, it was none the less a decision that cannot be faulted legally.

The constitutional architects had themselves evaded the question of citizenship for slaves. Ratification of the Constitution itself would not have taken place if slaves were to be counted as citizens, and the obvious political compromise in 1787 was to omit blacks as citizens but to strengthen their count for political representation in Congress. Although they could not vote, they were counted as three-fifths of a person for apportionment.

Chief Justice Taney, whatever else he may have felt about the cause of racial equality, decided this case *before* the Fourteenth Amendment was passed. He had no constitutional precedent to declare anyone a citizen who was not already a citizen of a state. If Missouri did not consider Dred Scott a citizen, entitled there to its rights, the United States could not. The Fourteenth Amendment, preceded by the Thirteenth, both solved and confused the question of citizenship and equal rights.

THE THIRTEENTH AMENDMENT

In the early days of the Republic the slavery issue pointedly intruded itself into nearly every other issue, surfacing constantly and challenging in unpredictable and subtle ways the perceptions and feelings of those who cried liberty loudest. Slavery was the largest skeleton in the closet of the confederacy and Republic, omnipresent and dormant, but not dealt with finally until 1865: 'Neither Slavery nor involuntary servitude, except as a punishment for crime whereof the party shall have been duly convicted, shall exist within the United States, or any place subject to their jurisdiction.' (Thirteenth Amendment) Thus, Lincoln's Emancipation Proclamation ending slavery by executive order did not free slaves who resided in those border states which did not secede from the Union. The Emancipation Proclamation was a military order, not a judicial statute. Lincoln was acting as commander-in-chief of the armed services. The Constitution, without the Thirteenth Amendment, still recognised slaves as property, to be counted in congressional representation, but having no voting privileges themselves.

Even before the proclamation, in 1862, Lincoln had signed an act ending slavery in the District of Columbia: the federal government was to buy the slaves at a price not above $200. He also asked Congress to recognise Haiti and Liberia, even providing free passage to those countries for freed slaves. A preliminary Emancipation Proclamation was published after a Cabinet meeting where members agreed to its contents, to take effect 1 January 1863. Its meaning was clear and unequivocal: 'All persons held as slaves within any state or designated part of a state, the people . . . shall be then thenceforward and forever free.' The boldness of the stroke disarmed enemies. But it also struck at the shareowners' wallets. Slaves were valued at that time as property worth about $3 billion (US). More than 1.3 million slaves had been emancipated by this event and other consequences of the war.

In 1864 Lincoln in an address to Congress suggested 'a proposed amendment to the Constitution, abolishing slavery throughout the United States'. Lincoln had the Senate safe for a vote, but the House was doubtful. He admitted Nevada into the Union with its added votes in Congress, and this helped to narrow the margin. Even Representative James Rollins, one of the largest slaveholders in Missouri, agreed to the proposed amendment and was to help persuade other congressional colleagues. The final vote for ratification passed by the slender margin of three with eight abstentions.

THE FOURTEENTH AMENDMENT

| Amendment V | . . . nor be deprived of life, liberty, or property without due process of law. |
| Amendment XIV | . . . nor shall any State deprive any person of life, liberty, or property, without due process of law. |

Why do these nearly identical statements appear in both amendments? According to Chief Justice John Marshall's decision in *Barron vs Baltimore*, the first eight amendments were not binding on the states, only the federal government. The Fourteenth Amendment extended the rights enunciated in the Fifth Amendment and made them binding on the states as well, and prohibited states from discriminating judicially, 'without due process of law'.

But the Fourteenth Amendment added another phrase not found elsewhere, upon which so many future Court decisions would be based: the controversial 'equal protection' clause: 'No State shall . . . deny to any person within its jurisdiction the equal protection of the laws.' The 'equal protection' clause was meant to prohibit *statutory* discrimination on the part of the states, just as the 'due process' clause was meant to prohibit *judicial* discrimination.

Raoul Berger (1979) makes a persuasive argument for the Supreme Court's misinterpretation of the meaning of the Fourteenth Amendment in its desegregation rulings. His thesis is that the framers of the Amendment did not intend that it should mean 'full protection' under all laws, but only 'equality' under 'civil' not political rights. These 'civil' rights, says Berger, were limited to life, liberty and property, and did not extend to voting, marriage and desegregation. His evidence is based on documentation from the committees and congressional debates on the Amendment from the 39th Congress which passed the Fourteenth Amendment on 13 June 1866. Berger explains in concluding his study:

> The suffrage-segregation decisions go beyond the assumption of powers 'not warranted' by the Constitution; they represent the arrogation of powers that the framers plainly *excluded*. The Court, it is safe to say, has flouted the will of the framers and substituted an interpretation in flat contradiction of the original design: to leave suffrage, segregation and other matters to State governance.

The Amendment framers, Berger argues, were attempting to prevent two kinds of laws in the states, one for blacks and one for whites. They were not trying to extend every kind of right universally to all. Berger's conclusion is that the Court overreached itself and read into an ambiguous clause meanings which its original drafters had not intended.

However, Berger's evidence is incomplete. He claims, for example, that the 39th Congress never intended suffrage or desegregation in framing the Fourteenth Amendment. Yet he has overlooked all the activities of the 39th Congress to determine the mind-set of these legislators. For example, he does not comment on Congress's measures to enlarge the Freedmen's Bureau, a bill which originated with the Senate Judiciary Committee. This bill of 1866, the year of the Fourteenth Amendment, placed the expanded powers of the Bureau squarely in the administration of the President, and under his military jurisidiction. The new power consisted of the establishment of school houses (a fact significant in and of itself for the purposes of this study); but more significantly, the bill granted the Bureau wide jurisdiction over civil and criminal cases: 'where equality in civil rights and status, and in the application of penalities was denied, or the denial thereof attempted, on account of race, color, or previous condition of servitude.' This bill was passed in January 1866, some six months *before* the passage of the Fourteenth Amendment.

As the debate on the Fourteenth Amendment was about to open, one issue was concerning most legislators: which 'states' would be admitted or readmitted to the Union, and what would be their representation in Congress? Apportionment of new House members was a keen issue in the House. In fact, as early as 22 January 1866, a constitutional amendment on apportionment was submitted from the Committee on Reconstruction to both Houses. These issues now constitute Sections 2, 3 and 4 of the Fourteenth Amendment, so they were not neglected, only incorporated with the concept of equality, 'equal protection' and 'due process'.

A bill was also submitted that proposed to apply the Amendment to the Southern 'states' *as the condition of their admission to representation in Congress*. It was fortunately not enacted, but its intent of coercion was nevertheless conveyed.

The Fourteenth Amendment in the popular mind was clearly a test for 'state' readmission. Tennessee's swift acceptance within a month had set a precedent. Does it not seem inconsistent that the Republicans who dominated Congress were prepared to recognise these 'states' still under martial law, even though they were not yet under any constitutional warranties? Why then did Congress submit for adoption the Fourteenth Amendment to those 'states' which were not yet constituted as states, that did not yet have legislatures representative of the people recognised by the federal government? It can only have been because the states knew that their admission into the Union was contingent upon their recognition of the Fourteenth Amendment. It was a subtle and unconstitutional form of bribery. But even more, it was a way Congress in 1867 could brush aside *executive* reconstruction and substitute *legislative* reconstruction.

No sooner were the autumn elections over, than a bill was introduced to extend suffrage to blacks in the District of Columbia. Congress reasoned that it could not expect the South to accept suffrage unless the federal government were to establish it also in the North. President Johnson vetoed, but was overridden, and suffrage was established in the District in January 1867.

I believe that the 39th Congress was attempting to gain control of reconstruction from the President and of the membership of the Congress itself through apportionment, suffrage and civil rights. The Fourteenth Amendment was only one part of that political process to defeat and humiliate Johnson, to ensure a Republican party majority and to expand the party political base in future Congresses.

In sum, the Fourteenth Amendment became the carrot held out by the 39th Congress as a way of admitting states into the Union; of possibly setting up Republican party states to create a permanent majority in Congress; and of wresting the initiative from the President so as to control legislatively the process of Reconstruction and the membership of Congress. These are the central issues of the 39th Congress, of which civil rights became the means.

5

Judicial Policy in Race and Schooling

We conclude that in the field of public education the doctrine of 'separate but equal' has no place. Separate educational facilities are inherently unequal.

Chief Justice Earl Warren
Brown vs Board of Education
17 May 1954

Digests of US Supreme Court decisions involving education now run to many volumes, and the cases decided since the late 1960s and 1970s have radically changed schooling procedures. Some are concerned with procedural matters and school finance and organisation. The more important and far-reaching changes, however, have occurred in church/state relationships in education, student and teacher and employee rights and the subject of this chapter, race discrimination. There are a variety of discriminatory schooling policies and practices rectified by the US Supreme Court: rulings on language, sex and religion, to name but a few. None, however, has caused as much social disruption and national trauma as the desegregation issue, especially since the Warren *Brown vs Board of Education* decision in 1954. I believe that race and schooling best illustrates the judicial side of the federal government in action.

Does the First Amendment right of freedom of speech and expression include the right to exclude individuals from a particular school? No, it violates the right of those excluded by denying them equality of educational opportunity. Can a voter initiative, expressing the collective right of a people to govern themselves, include the right to ban school busing? Not if it violates established constitutional privileges, ruled the Court. Does a state ballot initiative that limits a state court's power over desegregation meet the test of constitutionality? Yes, said the Court in the 1982 California decision.

The articulation of these and other decisions regarding desegregation and busing — and also prayers in schools, the teaching of evolution, and the banning of school books — reveals the strength of the independent judiciary and constitutional democracy. It also reveals the depth of the social, psychological and cultural divisions in American society. America as a nation has little stomach for a fully integrated society. Yet the past, if we know it, is prologue to the future. It is thus helpful to study the history of school segregation the better to understand a nation's heritage. 'It should go without saying', the Court said in *Brown II*, 'that the vitality of these constitutional principles cannot be allowed to yield simply because of disagreement with them.'

RESIDENCE AND RACE

Residence, not race, was the rule of thumb that guided the earliest American legal precedents for school attendance. Not until 1952 in a federal court in Delaware, in a decision used in the *Brown* case, did the *quality* of schooling become a determining factor for children attending school. One of the earliest instances of residential criteria for school attendance is in Massachusetts. The town of Stowe in 1805 wanted to expand its political jurisdiction by consolidating its school districts into one district. The law at the time was unspecific over geographic boundaries, so the school board named the individual families whose children could attend, regardless of where they lived. The court ruled against the schools, because the schools had not taken into account provision for new families who might move into the district, whose children would not be able to attend because their family names would not have been listed. As the system of free schools expanded, so did the kinds of children who wanted to attend. In 1849 the black parents of Susan Roberts went to court in Boston. School officials there had deliberately decided to segregate children by race. The regulation of the school board noted that, even though children are 'entitled to enter the schools nearest to their place of residence', this was not an absolute ruling and exceptions could be made. The exception was for race. The court upheld the school board's ruling and refused to order Susan Roberts' admission to the school nearer her place of residence. It directed her to remain in one of the two black schools. This is the first instance of court-ordered segregation. The court ruling had violated the commonly understood belief that children should attend their neighbourhood schools.

Segregation of schooling by race was not localised to Massachusetts. Deliberate segregation was more obvious in Albany, New York, in 1872. The public school districts had been created in the state of New York in 1812 and were dependent on property boundaries. Again, a black parent had brought suit to have his child admitted to the school nearest his place of residence. The school board had insisted that the child attend the black school, more distant from his home. There were many schools within the city and no statutory attendance areas. The court ruled that the school board had the authority to establish its own attendance boundaries.

In 1873 segregated schools existed everywhere in the United States. In Wilkes-Barre, Pennsylvania, in that year, however, there was an unusual instance of the court allowing a black child to attend a white school. The school board of Wilkes-Barre had segregated schools, even though there were too few children to attend the separate black schools. A black parent sued to allow his child to attend the nearer white school. The court found in his favour.

School gerrymandering, the deliberate and artful manipulation of school district boundaries and attendance lines in accordance with housing and residence patterns, usually already racially segregated, ensured the perpetuity of racial imbalance in the schools. School boards usually had standard criteria for school attendance boundaries: distances from home to school; convenience of transportation; topographical barriers; numbers of students; accessibility and safety. The *quality* of the educational programme was never a criterion until recent decades. The assumption was that schools were all equally good, not only within but *across* segregation.

Thus, except for race, the operational scheme and guide for admission to school systems became proximity to a child's home. However, the concept, though it was the assumed principle, was not tested legally. Clearly, black children were then excluded from the nearest schools simply because those schools had white children. Yet although black parents frequently had recourse to the courts, the courts themselves never established the principle of school assignment by proximity of residence to school. The concept of the neighbourhood school was used as the rationalisation to keep schools racially distinct. Whatever the slogan of neighbourhood school meant in the rhetoric of the day, its legal basis remained undefined. The concept of the neighbourhood school, however, failed to take root in the South principally because of the rural nature of communities. Schools for black children were not formed at all unless there were sufficient numbers to justify beginning a school.

What is evident from the legal history of schooling is that race altered the meaning of the common school. It was not common to all but only common to some. The history of schooling in America, then, is a history of dual and separate school systems. The segregation ideology grew with the growth of the schools.

Segregating by race was not limited to blacks and whites.

Congress had passed a law in 1905 which created a dual school system in Alaska: 'The schools specified and provided for in this act shall be devoted to the education of white children and children of mixed blood who lead a civilized life.' A court order in 1906 upheld the ruling of the school board in Sitka, Alaska, then the state capital, that excluded from public schools the children of three mixed-blood families who were partly American Indian. The argument the court used in its ruling was that the parents were not leading 'a civilized life'. The first plaintiff was a Presbyterian, wrote and spoke English and operated a local business, presumably according to civilised methods. The court said that 'civilization is more than a prosperous business, a trade, a house, white man's clothes, and membership in a church'. The phrase 'more than' was never specified. It was clearly race, but it was also residence. The children of the plaintiff did not live in the 'civilized' city of Sitka, but in the suburbs. Those who were ruling on the case did not deal with the issue of how a person becomes civilised. There were as yet no legal precedents that might have discouraged further segregation in the schools. School segregation was, after all, a well-established tradition.

It was not until the period after World War II that a few cases coming to the Supreme Court for review began to change the pattern for school segregation. Yet the first case was not about the Fourteenth Amendment and equal protection. It was about interstate travel.

Morgan was a passenger in the mid-1940s in a motor vehicle operated by the Commonwealth of Virginia. The bus went from Richmond through the district of Columbia to Maryland. Morgan, a black citizen, did not take a seat assignment given to him by the conductor in the section reserved for blacks, thereby violating a state code. The Supreme Court ruled:

As there is no federal act dealing with the separation of races in interstate transportation, we must decide the validity of this Virginia statute on the challenge that it interferes with commerce, as a matter of balance between the need for national uniformity in the regulations for interstate travel. It seems clear to us that seating arrangements for the different races in interstate motor travel requires a single, uniform rule to promote national travel. Consequently, we hold the Virginia statute in controversy invalid.

The first bastion in a long line of state statutes which regulated segregation of black and white had fallen. There would be others. But the irony was not lost on those who knew the history of the courts: it

71

was Homer Plessy who first had challenged the court on segregated transportation ruling, and he had lost. That decision apparently now had been reversed, not on the grounds of the Fourteenth Amendment but on interstate commerce. Would it then be possible that the court was willing to be challenged again on segregation in the schools based on the Fourteenth Amendment?

In 1947 the court ruled on two other cases, this time dealing with the right to buy and reside on property: one from Missouri and another from Michigan, where blacks had been denied the right to own or occupy real property by a restrictive agreement. Property-owners in an area had signed an agreement excluding 'people of the Negroid or Mongoloid Race' from buying their property or acting as tenants on it. The black petitioners had purchased some of this property through an agent unaware of the covenant against them. The white property-owners who had participated in the restrictive agreement brought suit.

The Supreme Court argued that state had brought its power to bear in attempting to enforce the restrictive order.

> We hold that in granting judicial enforcement of the restrictive agreements in these cases, the States have denied petitioners the equal protection of the laws, and that, therefore, the action of the State courts cannot stand. We have noted that freedom from discrimination by the States in the enjoyment of property rights was among the basic objectives sought to be effectuated by the framers of the Fourteenth Amendment. That such discrimination has occurred in these cases is clear . . . Equal protection of the laws is not achieved through indiscriminate imposition of inequalities.

These cases, again though not strictly dealing with education, are none the less significant because they were used as precedents in later cases which did concern education.

ADMISSION AND RACE

Lloyd Gaines, a prospective candidate for law school at the University of Missouri, was black. He was denied admission in 1936 after he had graduated with a BA from Lincoln University, a college for blacks, solely because of his colour. In neighbouring states, Kansas, Nebraska, Illinois and Iowa, non-residents were admitted in the state universities. But in Missouri it was contrary to the constitution, laws and public policy of the state to admit a negro as a student in the University of Missouri.

The court ruled, in *Gaines vs Canada* that:

> The basic consideration is not as to what sort of opportunities other states provide, or whether they are as good as those in Missouri, but as to what opportunities Missouri itself furnishes to white students and denies to negroes solely upon the ground of color. The question here is not of a duty of the State to supply legal training, or of the quality of the training which it does supply, but of its duty when it provides such training to furnish it to the residents of the state upon the basis of an equality of right. By the operation of the laws of Missouri a privilege has been created for white law students which is denied to negroes by reason of their race.

The case of Lloyd Gaines is the first which asked for equal educational protection under the laws and the Fourteenth Amendment. It is also the first against an educational institution on the grounds of discrimination.

In 1949 McLaurin, a black citizen of Oklahoma, holder of a master's degree, sought admission to the state university. He sought to become a doctoral student in education. His application was denied solely because of his colour, a law based on Oklahoma statute. Oklahoma law permitted black students to attend white institutions, but required that the instruction be given on a segregated basis. When McLaurin was admitted later, he was segregated by having a separate desk in the library, a separate table in the cafeteria, and segregated instruction. Chief Justice Vinson, writing the majority opinion, said:

> We conclude that the conditions under which this appelant is required to receive his education deprive him of his personal and present right to the equal protection of the laws . . . Appellant, having been admitted to a state-supported graduate school, must receive the same treatment at the hands of the state as students of other races. State-imposed restrictions which produce such inequalities cannot be sustained.

Lastly, the case of *Hawkins vs Board of Control of Florida* is perhaps unprecedented in the annals of desegregating higher education institutions. Virgil Hawkins had applied to admission to the all-white law school at the University of Florida. He was denied admission in 1949 because he was black. The State of Florida, through its higher education board, kept petitioning the Supreme Court for a delay in implementing the court's decision that he be admitted. Although the case came before the Supreme Court three times, because of the ten-year delay Virgil Hawkins was never able to enter law school. The court had found him relief, but the delay had tested his patience.

SCHOOLING AND RACE

The Supreme Court decision allowing 'separate but equal' schools did not arise from a school or parent plaintiff. It arose because Homer Plessy, a passenger on a train in Louisiana, sat in the section of the train reserved for whites. He had been seated in the black passenger section but insisted on going into the white passenger section, contrary at the time to Louisiana law. 'Neither in the information nor the plea was his particular race or color averred' said Mr Justice Henry B. Brown in the court's opinion. The opinion continued:

The petition for the writ of prohibition averred that the petitioner was seven-eights Causasian and one-eighth African blood; that the mixture of colored blood was not discernible in him, and that he was entitled to every right, privilege and immunity secured to citizens of the United States of white race.

The attempt of this suit was to force the judgment of the court on the constitutionality of the equality of blacks and whites according to both the Thirteenth and Fourteenth Amendments to the Constitution.

Mr Justice Brown found that the decision of the Louisiana court was 'reasonable':

Gauged by this standard [acceptance among the people] we cannot say that a law which authorizes or even requires the separation of the two races in public conveyances is unreasonable, or more obnoxious to the Fourteenth Amendment than the acts of Congress requiring separate schools for colored children in the District of Columbia, the constitutionality of which does not seem to have been questioned.

He decided against the plaintiff, Plessy, and continued with a short discourse against the argument that social prejudices can be overcome by legislation: 'Legislation is powerless to eradicate racial instincts or to abolish distinctions based upon physical differences.'

Plessy vs Ferguson contributed to the continuing philosophy of 'separate but equal', the dual and segregated system of schooling. Though separate schools were rarely equal in quality, facilities, financing, or any other dimension. The pattern of segregated schooling was nearly everywhere confirmed by state statutes. There was one single dissenter in the eight-to-one count in the Plessy decision. Mr Justice Harlan, in his minority opinion, wrote: 'Our Constitution is color-blind.' That minority report deserves close attention.

Justice Harlan's dissenting opinion in the Plessy decision was consistent with his other opinions, which also were always in the minority on issues concerning the Fourteenth Amendment. He had gone to the heart of the matter by pointing out that the Louisiana statute was an attempt to write racial supremacy into law.

But in view of the Constitution, in the eye of the law, there is in this country no superior, no dominant, ruling class of citizens. There is no caste here. Our Constitution is color-blind, and neither knows nor tolerates classes among citizens. The present decision . . . will encourage the belief that it is possible, by means of state enactments, to defeat the beneficient purposes which the people of the United States had in view when they adopted the recent amendment of the Constitution . . . The destinies of the two races in this country are indissolubly linked together, and the interests of both require that the common government of all shall not permit the seeds of race hatred to be planted under the sanction of law.

His dissent is a moving testimonial. He wanted 'equality before the law of all the citizens of the United States without regard to race'. In spite of his dissent, however, the time had not yet come. Today his opinion prevails.

Do separate schools for blacks and white provide equality of opportunity? It was always contended that because they were separated they were indeed equal in educational provision. The test case arose in Delaware in 1952 in *Belton vs Gebhart*. The real constitutional issue was whether or not the plaintiffs' rights were being violated under the Fourteenth Amendment. There were two actions. Black residents of Claymount School District in New Castle County were refused admission to that high school, which was all-white, solely because of their colour and ancestry. They were permitted, however, to enter Howard High School and Carver Vocational School, both schools for blacks. These schools were about nine miles distant. The state code had directed that there be separate and free schools for blacks and whites. The second action was whether or not the facilities and educational opportunities offered to blacks were inferior to those offered for whites.

The plaintiffs contended that legally enforced segregation in education prevented their children and others similarly placed from receiving equal treatment. They produced many expert witnesses in education, sociology, psychology, psychiatry and anthropology. The judge was obviously impressed, for he ruled:

> I conclude from the testimony that in our Delaware society, State-imposed segregation in education itself results in Negro children, as a class, receiving educational opportunities which are substantially inferior to those available to white children otherwise similarly situated.

Judge Seitz was determining whether or not the 'separate but equal' doctrine could be applied to elementary and secondary schools, knowing that it prevailed on a personal basis in admission criteria for higher education. It was an open question, because even though the *Brown* case was actually at the time pending in the Supreme Court, there were no precedents. The judge surmised that segregation was not allowed at the lower school levels at any rate: 'In other words, by implication, The Supreme Court of the United States has said a separate but equal test can be applied, at least below the college level.' Judge Seitz continued by indicating that the Supreme Court had not yet decided on whether some schools are inferior to others. But he believed that if they were, the principle of 'separate but equal' would be violated:

> The cold hard fact is that the State in this situation discriminates against Negro children. I conclude that with respect to teacher training, pupil-teacher ratio, extracurricular activities, physical plants and aesthetic considerations, the Howard-Carver School is inferior to Claymont under the 'separate but equal' test.

His decision was, therefore, that the black children would have to be admitted to the white school since that school was admittedly and by means of all known criteria superior to the black schools.

BROWN VS BOARD OF EDUCATION

The US Supreme Court could have heard any number of cases on the subject of admitting blacks to white schools. Petitions came from South Carolina, Virginia, Delaware and Kansas. In each case, parents had sought their children's admission to the public schools in their community. They had been denied admission to the white schools by state laws which permitted segregation by race.

Except in Delaware a three-judge federal district court had denied the plaintiffs, in each instance citing the *Plessy vs Ferguson* decision which allowed for separate but equal schools and treatment. In Delaware, although the federal district court granted the admissibility of the Plessy doctrine, it permitted the black plaintiffs to be entered in the white schools because the white schools were admittedly of better quality. It is the first acknowledgement by the courts of degrees of quality in the schools, especially of superiority of white schools over black schools.

The Supreme Court took over two years on this decision, and heard arguments on circumstances surrounding the adoption of the Fourteenth Amendment, its consideration in Congress, its ratification by the states, existing practices in racial discrimination and views of opponents and proponents. The court noted that an analysis of the history of the amendment was inconclusive with respect to segregated schools at that time.

There had been many attempts to make black schools 'equal' to those of whites in teacher salaries, facilities, curricula, buildings and other measurable criteria. But the court chose instead to go beyond the equalisation of materials to the effect of segregated schools on American life. The majority opinion, unanimous, was written by Mr Chief Justice Warren:

> Today, education is perhaps the most important function of state and local governments. Compulsory school attendance laws and the great expenditures for education both demonstrate our recognition of the importance of education to our democratic society . . . In these days, it is doubtful that any child may reasonably be expected to succeed in life if he is denied the opportunity of any education. Such an opportunity, where the state has undertaken to provide it, is a right which must be made available to all on equal terms. We come then to the question presented: Does segregation of children in public schools, solely on the basis of race, even though the physical facilities and other 'tangible' factors

may be equal, deprive the children of the minority group of equal educational opportunities? We believe that it does.

The court continues by rejecting the philosophy which led to the decision of *Plessy vs Ferguson*: 'Whatever may have been the extent of psychological knowledge at the time of *Plessy v. Ferguson*, this finding is amply supported by modern authority. Any language in *Plessy v. Ferguson* contrary to this finding is rejected.' Lastly, the court concludes with the statements so often quoted as the first major decision ending segregated schooling:

We conclude that in the field of public education the doctrine of 'separate but equal' has no place. Separate educational facilities are inherently unequal. Therefore, we hold that the plaintiffs and others similarly situated for whom the actions have been brought are, by reason of the segregation complained of, deprived of the equal protection of the laws guaranteed by the Fourteenth Amendment.

The court had spoken. A century of unequal schooling treatment had been adjudicated. But a trail of litigation was still to follow detailing the methods for desegregating, prompting timetables, bus transportation routes, petitioning for relief, in some cases leading to the closing of schools. But the court, in its Implementation Decision (1955), laid on school authorities the responsibility for carrying out the decision of the court.

Full implementation of these constitutional principles may require solution of varied local school problems. School authorities have the primary responsibility for elucidating, assessing, and solving these problems; courts will have to consider whether the action of school authorities constitutes good faith implementation of the governing constitutional principles.

The court had anticipated disagreement and noted simply that it had ruled and would not countenance non-compliance.

The court had also anticipated that there would be definite time-lags in implementing its decision to desgregate, and so it commented in the Implementation Decision that desegregating the schools should be done quickly. Despite these calls for compliance within reasonable time, *de facto* segregation still existed years later in many urban centres, and the boundaries dividing cities, town and counties, and

78

in some instances states, had become the new lines where segregation began or ended.

Moreover, the court had ruled on a 'right' that neither the Constitution itself nor any of its amendments had before specified: '[Educational opportunity] is a right which must be made available to all on equal terms.'

The principle of officially segregated education did not end with the *Brown* decision. The court had acknowledged its lack of enforcement power, and left with the federal courts the problem of solving 'the varied local school problems'. But the court had assumed that because it had passed judgment there would be 'prompt and reasonable start' to fulfil the constitutional definition. It was a correct legal assumption but a poor social one. Federal judges did not easily acquiesce where popular sentiment clearly ran counter, and local authorities did not move with any alacrity to desegregate.

When in 1957 the Governor of Arkansas called out the national guard to prevent black students from attending Little Rock Central High School because of the possibility of threatened violence — though he did not consult school officials who had prepared for an orderly transition — hysteria, panic and fear rippled through the nation. For President Eisenhower the time for fulfilling his constitutional oath had come. He nationalised the Arkansas guard and ordered them to escort the black students into school.

Earlier, a federal judge had authorised an order permitting the postponment of desegregation because of the threat of violence. The Supreme Court in *Cooper vs Aaron* rejected this order and instead ordered the students to be admitted to school. The wording of this order is unequivocal:

> Law and order are not here to be preserved by depriving the Negro children of their constitutional rights. [These] can neither be nullified openly and directly by state legislators or State executive or judicial officers, nor nullified indirectly by them through evasive schemes for segregation.

The *Cooper vs Aaron* decision in 1958, perhaps even more than the *Brown* decision, blocked on the legal front the segregationist movement which had attempted to nullify the *Brown* decision.

The activities of the late 1950s and early 1960s were a tug-of-war between the three branches of government on enforcement of the desegregation decision. The executive was clearly in sympathy with local school problems and encouraged delays. In fact, there was no enforcement power at all from either the executive or legislative branches during the Eisenhower or Kennedy Administrations. Only under the Johnson Administration, by the passage of the Civil Rights Act, did the whole of the federal government appear to agree finally on the strategy of desegregation.

As the composition of the Court itself changed, and as successive chief executives stated their policies for administration of schooling programmes, schools were sometimes sent conflicting signals. Congress added fuel to the fire when in 1979 it narrowly defeated a drive for an antibusing constitutional amendment, falling several votes short of a majority on the floor of the House. The motion had been forced out of Committee by a discharge petition signed by a majority of the House members, a rarely used parliamentary tactic. As a result of divided opinion, the 1980 election campaign used increasingly strident tones and rhetoric as more and more communities were affected.

BUSING, RACE AND STATE POWER

Can a plebiscite by direct ballot, and can a people by means of elected representatives, forbid a state court to enforce desegregative busing intended to end segregation? Can an elected local school board defend its busing programme from state attacks to curtail it? The questions raised here were central to the arguments heard by the US Supreme Court in 1982 in *Crawford vs Board of Education of the City of Los Angeles*, and in *Washington vs Seattle School District*.

Los Angeles City Schools in 1980 included 562 schools with 650,000 students in 711 square miles. The racial composition of the schools had altered significantly between the time desegregation litigation first began in 1963, until 1970 when the trial court found the Los Angeles schools in substantial violation of both the federal and state constitutions, until the new trial in 1980 and 1982. Both the Hispanic and Asian school populations had doubled, while the white school population was more than halved in proportion. From 1968 to 1980 the black school population remained relatively stable.

The trial court in 1970 in Los Angeles ordered the city schools to prepare a desegregation plan for immediate use. The California Supreme Court, on appeal, affirmed, but on the basis of the equal protection clause of the *state* constitution. The appeal court noted that: 'State school boards . . . bear a constitutional obligation to take reasonable steps to alleviate segregation in the public schools, whether the segregation be *de facto* or *de jure* in origin.'

Once the plan went into effect in the autumn of 1978, all parties agreed that it was disappointing and unsatisfactory. Alternative plans were under consideration in 1979 when the California plebiscite ratified Proposition I, which became an amendment to the state constitution. It said in part:

No court of this state may impose upon the State of California or any public entity, board, or official, any obligation or responsibility with respect to the use of pupil assignment or pupil transportation; (1) except to remedy a specific violation of the Equal Protection Clause of the 14th Amendment to the United States Constitution, and (2) unless a federal court would be permitted under federal decisional law to impose that obligation or responsibility upon such party to remedy the specific violation of the Equal Protection Clause.

Once Proposition I had attained a two-thirds vote of each house of the state legislature, and received a majority vote throughout the state, the Los Angeles schools requested the Superior Court to halt mandatory busing. The California Court of Appeal ruled definitively that Proposition I was now constitutional.

The US Supreme Court affirmed the Appeal Court's interpretation. In effect, Proposition I forbade the state court from ordering busing. Justice Powell noted for the majority:

Proposition I in no way purports to limit the power of state courts to remedy the effects of intentional segregation . . . The Proposition simply removes one means of achieving the state created right to desegrated education. School districts retain the obligation to alleviate segregation regardless of cause. And the state courts still may order desegregation measures other than pupil school assignment or pupil transportation.

Justice Marshall, writing the lone dissent, found that Proposition I had decided racial overtones, an argument the original petitioners had used.

Proposition I works an unconstitutional re-allocation of state power by depriving California courts of the ability to grant meaningful relief to those seeking to vindicate the state's guarantee against *de facto* segregation in the public schools.

After the adoption of Proposition I, the only method of

enforcing against a recalcitrant school board the state constitutional duty to eliminate racial isolation is to petition either the state legislature or the electorate as a whole.

Seattle School District had enacted a comprehensive desegregation plan in 1978 that made extensive use of mandatory busing. The Seattle schools administered 112 schools with 54,000 students, of whom 37 per cent were minority students. Segregated housing patterns throughout the city had created racially imbalanced schools which the district had historically taken steps to correct. The courts even found in 1978 that the Seattle plan: 'Had substantially reduced the number of racially imbalanced schools in the district and has substantially reduced the percentage of minority students in those schools which remain racially imbalanced.'

In late 1978 the State of Washington passed initiative 350 by a substantial margin. This initiative was drafted to terminate mandatory busing for the purpose of racial integration. It further prohibited schools from requiring students to attend any school other than a 'neighbourhood' school. It set out many exceptions to this requirement, but not any that related to racial reasons.

The District Court held Washington's Initiative 350 unconstitutional 'because it permits busing for non-racial reasons, but forbids it for racial reasons'. The US Court of Appeals reaffirmed this opinion by concluding that the initiative: 'Both creates a constitutionally-suspect racial classification and radically restructures the political process of Washington by allowing a state-wide majority to usurp traditional local authority over local school board educational policies.' The US Supreme Court upheld the Appeal Court's decision.

The Supreme Court argued that Initiative 350 as ratified would have worked a special hardship on minorities, placing a different state decision-making apparatus over desegregation busing only. The Court's decision was not based on whether or not the state had the authority to intervene, but whether or not it did so in this instance to circumvent provisions of the Fourteenth Amendment and other court interpretations regarding school desegregation.

CONCLUSION

Once the *Brown* decision had overruled *Plessy vs Ferguson* and decided that separate schools for blacks and whites were unconstitutional, it also extended in subsequent decisions its jurisdiction to the implementation and monitoring of its decision. Now the basis was extended to First Amendment rights 'to petition the government for a redress of grievances' based on decisions made under the Fourteenth Amendment. This was done in the *Tinker* decision in 1969. The Court intervened in what previously had been state and local school authority and decided instead on behalf of the student's constitutional rights of equal protection and due process. It defined the student as a 'person' under the Constitution and thus eligible for constitutional relief if privileges have been abused.

The 'right to an education' debate came to the Court's attention and it decided, in *San Antonio vs Rodrigues*, that there was no constitutional guarantee to an education, that education was not a 'fundamental' right like freedom of speech. But the *Goss* decision settled that issue by establishing education as one of the *property* rights ('life, liberty, and property') and thus protected by the due process clause. The majority opinion of the Court in the *Goss* case (*Goss vs Lopez*, 1975), moreover, held school board members liable for abridgement of constitutional rights of students. Henceforward, the Court determined, they were no longer immune from prosecution or damages.

The Supreme Court does not appear to be anxious to intervene in the daily operations of schooling. If this is clearly a contemporary legal and educational phenomenon, it is because the Court is now finding that constitutional privileges are extended to students, and that nowhere ought those rights and privileges to be more protected than in the schools, and in its rules and regulations. The fact that the schools have had the presumed prerogative of monitoring themselves in the past no longer holds water.

There was a time after *Brown* when social science research and methodology did not have data available on the harmful effects of segregated schools. The only large-scale social science research on blacks in America was by the Swedish sociologist, Gunnar Myrdal (1941). Now that there *is* a convincing body of evidence, the education profession tends to disbelieve it, attacking it on methodological grounds. The paradox is that the deliberate intervention of the Courts and the Congress in the desegregation controversy seems to be unacceptable, regardless of the social good to be derived.

This is no doubt true because of the pervasive acceptance based on common tradition that local school problems were under exclusive local control. It is regrettable that politicians, to the detriment of improved civic and constitutional understanding, play on these politically responsive chords of federal intervention in local affairs. The problem of control is of course vertical as well as horizontal, in schooling as in other domestic and constitutional problems. By and large, school officials are sadly misinformed about the role of the judiciary in schooling. Conversely, judges and legal officials appear to be limited in their knowledge of the operation and maintenance of schools. The politics of these two governmental systems, their processes, their peculiar languages and their professional practices are now interlocked in a common problem over the rights of education.

It is difficult to place the whole problem of desegregation and busing in a national perspective, even a judicial one, without a consideration of other factors, such as the local history of race relations, the success of desegregation implementation and even the internal conditions of schools themselves, particularly the school leadership. Recent evidence suggests that desegregation is positively associated with racial tolerance and that students benefit most if introduced to it at an earlier age.

The courts have been created and expanded to resolve conflicts peacefully. Increasingly, courts have been called upon because of the partial paralysis of other governmental structures to deal honestly with acute social concerns. Busing and segregation in public facilities have now been absorbed in a longer list of court battles: gun control, abortion, the worth of certain pharmaceutical products, labour/management relations. Individuals as well as institutions seem to have lost the ability to reconcile their differences without arbitration and the decisive influence of special interest groups. Apart from the polarisation of society and the long history of discrimination in schooling, prejudice is still found in good measure, and the gap may even be widening.

Chief Justice Burger said in the *Milliken vs Bradley* decision regarding desegregation in Detroit:

> Of course, no state law is above the Constitution. School district lines and the present laws with respect to local school control are not sacrosanct and if they conflict with the Fourteenth Amendment federal courts have a duty to prescribe appropriate remedies.

So for all the 'invasion' of the courts into school supervision and local autonomy — from metropolitan busing and desegregation, to school discipline, dress codes and privacy — the law is mute on whether or not the courts can intervene. The dilemma for education is how to raise awareness in a new generation of American students of constitutional privileges that a few years ago no one knew they had; and in a new generation of educators that schools do not have complete local autonomy over students. Equality of schooling, whatever was thought in 1866 and 1868, is now an American reality

Part Three: The US Congress and Education

Let every state reserve its sovereign right of directing its own internal affairs, but give to Congress the sole right of conducting the general affairs of the continent.

Noah Webster
Sketches of American Policy, 1785

6

The Evolution of Federal Education Legislation

On an otherwise indistinguishable mound the Capitol rises with stately splendour, commanding the sweeping view of federal Washington that designer Pierre L'Enfant intended. Its dome catches the first hint of morning sunshine and the last rays of the day's light. Its massive size staggers the perceptual vision of anyone seeing it for the first time, and it easily rivals the Palace of Versailles or St Peter's Basilica in architectural awesomeness. As human monuments go, it is comparatively new among the structures erected to do justice to man's fallibility and his grandeur.

But it is its interior, not its grandiose exterior, that has shaped the American character. This tremendous Capitol edifice can only act as a reminder of the struggles to maintain liberty, and of the necessity to preserve law as the foundation of democratic life. Fittingly, no natural landmark exists to dwarf in presence the debates, discussions, hearings, compromises and political alliances of the chosen representatives of the body politic who work there.

Congress is the voice of the people, the legislator of the public's laws, the forum of agreement and dissent of the democracy's diversified interests. What are the origins of Congress, and what about it can illuminate our analysis of education?

LEGISLATIVE TRADITION AND CUSTOMS

In a sense, the origins of the legislative body, even deliberating about education, are as old as democracy itself. Aristotle wrote:

> It is clear that there should be legislation about education and that it should be conducted on a public system . . . What constitutes

education and what is the proper way to be educated? At present there are differences of opinion as to the proper tasks to be set; for all peoples do not agree as to the things that the young ought to learn . . . nor is it clear whether their studies should be regulated more with regard to intellect or with regard to character. And confusing questions arise out of the education that actually prevails, and it is not clear whether the pupils should practice pursuits that are practically useful, or morally edifying, or higher accomplishments — for all these views have won the support of some judges.

(Politics VIII, 2)

Closer to our own time, the tradition of a parliamentary body making laws suited to the day comes from England. King John was well aware of the peculiarity of the times when he signed the *Magna Carta* on the field at Runnymede in 1215, for his hand had been forced, and he did it only to prevent another rebellion by the landed barons. The presence of the representatives from the shires was an anomaly, the political innovation of the day, and it changed forever the concept of law from a regal to a legal status.

Yet resistance to kingly prerogative was to continue. When Charles I went to war with France and Spain, Parliament refused him resources to carry out his enterprise. Charles had to engage in extra-legal subterfuges, such as borrowing from his loyal subjects without Parliament's approval. Parliament cited the supremacy of the written word in the *Magna Carta* in its *Petition of Right*, and gave the king notice that he was extending his legal rights. Charles did what monarchs were expected to do: he dismissed Parliament, and for eleven years conveniently forgot to recall it. However, in 1640 he had to summon the lawmakers because the country was near insolvency, and trustworthy troops were not available. Parliament immediately passed a law requiring parliamentary meetings whether the king wanted them or not. Civil war was at hand.

By the time Cromwell had raised the people's army, the Rump Parliament was reasserting old beliefs such as 'the People are, under God, the original of all just power'. Thus, they, as collective representatives of the people, could even condemn a king.

When Charles was beheaded that January morning in 1649 on a scaffold outside his banqueting hall at Whitehall, more than a royal head fell. The concept of monarchy fell with it. A stronger idea arose: that the people are supreme in their role of deciding their destiny. It is this English concept of representative government, still fresh within the memories of the grandfathers and great-grandfathers of the constitutional architects, that will serve as perspective in our present analysis of how Congress influences educational policy.

'All legislative powers herein granted shall be vested in a Congress of the United States, which shall consist of a Senate and House of Representatives.' (Article I) Congress convenes a session in January of each odd-numbered year and continues, for two years, regardless of other special, regular or extraordinary sessions held. Under Article II, Section 3 a president may 'on extraordinary occasions' convene either the House or Senate or the whole Congress. Once assembled, however, Congress is not limited to the topic which the President requests.

Congressmen are elected by popular vote on the first Tuesday after the first Monday in November in the even-numbered years. The qualifications for voters in congressional elections are for the most part identical with those for voters in state elections, since the Constitution provides for the adopting of state provisions among the electorate. Senators, on the other hand, were not originally elected by popular vote but by state legislators. Popular vote of senators was only introduced in 1913 by the Seventeenth Amendment.

Only in recent times has the 'one man, one vote' phrase become a reality. Redistricting and reapportionment caused political consternation in House elections, particularly in 1968, but reaffirmed the prevailing democratic belief that there be equal population representation among the voting public in the House. Only the House is affected by population. According to the Constitution, each state has at least one representative. The actual size of the House, however, is determined by Congress, and there have been demands that the size of the House be reduced, but without avail. According to law, the membership is indefinitely fixed at 435. The business of Congress is the making of laws that regulate the national life. This is accomplished by introducing a bill or a measure and seeking its enactment by majority vote. 'Bill' is the term for a measure or proposal introduced in either the House or Senate. It becomes an 'Act' when one of the branches of Congress agrees to pass it on. It is then ordered to be printed as an Act by the House passing it. Popular understanding of an Act is the passage of a measure by both Houses. It becomes a law when the President signs it.

The stages of a bill differ in each house. In the House, a member places a measure in the 'hopper', a box on the clerk's desk. In the Senate, a Senator waits for recognition from the President of the Senate, the Vice-President of the United States, and introduces the bill on the floor. The bill is then referred to a select or standing committee, and the committee in turn reports its progress back to the floor, unless the bill has been reassigned to a subcommittee, in which case it is reported also to the full committee.

The bill is considered in the Committee of the whole of either the House or Senate and there is general debate and the reading of any amendments. There is a second and even a third reading, and finally a vote taken to decide passage or defeat. If originated in the House, the bill is then sent to the Senate, where it is again assigned to a committee. Differences can be settled in conference commitees composed of members of both Houses. If agreement is reached, the Act becomes enrolled on parchment paper by the initiating House. Many laws are specifically limited to a set number of years. Depending on congressional evaluation, further legislative life is either extended or withdrawn. The US statute books are littered with the remains of former education legislation.

The most common form of legislative change is an amendment, the rewording of times, dates, conditions and allocations. Hardly any law intended for education has not thus undergone tampering. Many former laws which once existed on their own have become amendments to more popularly accepted education acts, or parts of related legislation.

There is no guarantee that an act will be renewed simply because it has brought into existence a whole bureaucratic machinery: national advisory councils, national clearing-houses, state advisory councils, experimental and demonstration centres.

Finally, an Act can be 'sabotaged' by being denied appropriation, as was the International Education Act of 1966.

From 1974, Congress wrote into many education laws provision for legislative vetoes by one or other chamber: a technique to overturn actions by executive agencies. In what may become the most significant judicial decision of the 1980s, the US Supreme Court struck down this practice. When the Supreme Court vetoed the legislative veto in 1983, there were over 200 such statutes written into laws. There were at least four in education.

The Supreme Court decision noted that the legislative veto provisions were inconsistent with the Constitution, which requires that both houses passed on legislation, that the President sign and that a two-thirds majority of Congress be needed to overturn the President's veto. The wording of the Court's opinion defines even more carefully the lines separating the powers of the three branches of the federal government. What the Court said, in effect, was that the power of veto belongs to the President, not the Congress:

> The President's participation in the legislative process was to pro-
> tect the executive branch from Congress and to protect the whole
> people from improvident laws. The division of the Congress into
> two distinctive bodies assures that the legislative power would be
> exercised only after opportunity for full study and debate in separate
> settings. The President's unilateral veto power, in turn, was limited
> by the power of two-thirds of both houses of Congress to overrule
> a veto, thereby precluding final arbitrary action by one person . . .
> We hold that the congressional veto . . . is unconstitutional.

The use of the legislative veto arose chiefly during the Nixon
Administration, especially in fights with Congress over the war powers
during the Vietnam war, over impoundment by Nixon of monies
authorised by Congress and over control of regulatory agencies.
Although the use of the legislative veto in education was minimal,
it is now only a historical footnote to the way Congress writes laws.

The process by which Congress considers the administration of
federal education programmes it has legislated and for which it has
appropriated money is called *oversight*. These special hearings on the
management of each act by the executive are held annually shortly
after the fiscal year begins. They are crucial in aiding Congress in
determining the life frame of existing legislation and a probable
appropriation for the upcoming fiscal year.

> In framing a government which is to be administered by men over
> men, the great difficulty lies in this: You must first enable the
> government to control the governed; and in the second place, oblige
> it to control itself. A dependence on the people is no doubt the
> primary control on the governnent; but experience has taught
> mankind the necessity of auxiliary precautions.

In number 51 of the *Federalist Papers* (Ruttand, 1977) Madison
was attempting to persuade reluctant states and individuals that the
branches of government would maintain 'in practice the necessary
partition of power' among themselves but also that government would
have to have checks on itself.

The *General Accounting Office* (GAO) is Congress's check on congressional expenditures and over the executive branch's administration of funds. Its original legal charter is contained in the Treasury

Act of 1789, but the office was created by the Budget and Accounting Act of 1921. Its most recent legislation is in the General Accounting Act of 1980. The GAO assists materially in congressional oversight responsibilities. It has a non-partisan role, sometimes assisting in drafting legislation. However, its principal role in relation to education is in its review and evaluation of funded programmes. GAO has broad powers of audit and has the right, including the power of *subpoena*, of access to documents of any kind from other government agencies. It investigates all matters relating to the distribution and acceptance of federal funds and checks to see if they are spent as Congress authorised. GAO has the legal authority to check on government itself, as Madison suggested, as well as on any organisation which accepts federal money. One responsibility is the evaluation of education entitlement programmes, which creates special problems for GAO, since its goal is to reduce the waste, fraud and abuse so often used in campaign slogans. GAO's problem is that the evaluation of programmes is often a neglected concern, not undertaken until the project has ended.

One of the most extraordinary examples of congressional evaluation of federal education occurred in the mid-1960s. Edith Green, then chair of the Special Subcommittee of the House Committee on Education and Labor, mounted extensive evaluations of executive managed educational programmes. Throughout the 89th Congress she was relentless in pursuing administrative mismanagement. She requested the Comptroller General's Office to conduct an investigation of the Student Loan programme. Although this GAO investigation did not find any instances of misappropriation of funds, it did find several irregularities and numerous examples of mismanagement.

In fairness to the Office of Education during the mid-1960s, this was a period of extensive and unprecedented expansion, both numerically and qualitatively, of programmes and personnel. It was a time when the Elementary and Secondary Education Act was first administered. It was a time when the effects of the Civil Rights Act were becoming known and managed, and the political implications felt. It was a time of staggering appropriations increase. At issue here is not whether or not there was administrative mismanagement, or if there was, to what degree, but that the legislative role in actual programme management was expanded to an unprecedented extent. Edith Green went so far as to solicit education views directly from educators. She sent under the auspices of her subcommittee, a national questionnaire to state school chiefs, administrators and all school principals. Throughout her congressional tenure, she took an active hand in monitoring conduct of legislated education policies. In other words, she became an unauthorised part of the executive function of government, not just the legislature.

PERIODS OF CONGRESSIONAL HISTORY IN EDUCATION

The history of congressional intent in education in the years since independence has evolved, I believe, through six thematically distinct periods. Some of these stages overlap, although they do not appear to duplicate each other, except where an act increases the funding authorisation or appropriation. I believe that in this evolution the imprint of Congress in federal educational history has roughly corresponded with the nation's evolving and expanding domestic needs.

Land (1785-1896)

Congress's first dealings in education came prior to the Constitution and the creation of the national government. The land ordinance of 1785, as we saw earlier, provided that land be set aside in each township for the establishment of schools. The Northwest Ordinance of 1787 stated: 'Religion, morality and knowledge, being necessary to good government and the happiness of mankind, the means of education shall forever be encouraged.' The Ordinance did not actually bestow anything. All it did was to bless any educational effort. But education was quite clearly linked, as a subordinate feature, to the study of religion and morality and instruction in the faith, church and school being nearly always the same building.

This early characteristic of Congress's role in education is of grants of land. Congress made generous donations of both purchased and conscripted land for educational purposes whenever a new territory applied for statehood and entry into the Union: in Ohio in 1802, Illinois in 1818, Ohio in 1821, Michigan in 1837, Oregon in 1848 and Utah in 1896. The Morrill Land Grant Act in 1862, and later in 1890, provided land for agricultural and mechanical colleges: the first incursion of the federal government, apart from military colleges, into higher education.

A study in 1890 for the then US Bureau of Education pointed out that the concept of land grants was popularly accepted practice. The idea evolved from monastic land grants, and it was from the monasteries and the training of clerics that the first universities in

Western culture had their origin. In the territories, prior to statehood, the federal government gave direct support to education, as it did to Alaska before statehood. Some universities, such as Howard and Hampton Institute, were directly established by the federal government.

Thus, the federal government initiated the support for schools with a grant of land and the churches provided support and maintenance.

Veterans and manpower (1865-1958)

This second period of federal educational policy development and the chronicle of congressional action marks a significant shift. The emphasis turns to direct benefits to individuals in education. The largest and most effective programme initiated by the federal government has been the GI Bill.

The emphasis away from school allocation to individual allocation of educational benefits avoided the controversy that nearly sabotaged the Elementary and Secondary Education Act of 1965: the awarding of grants to parochial schools.

Here is a selective listing of the education programmes for veterans:

1865 Freedman's Bureau to aid Negro education (later to become Howard University)
1916 National Defense Act authorised ROTC
1918 Vocational Rehabilitation Act for World War I veterans
1944 The GI Bill
1952 Aid to veterans from Korea
1956 Korean GI Bill extended aid to orphans of veterans
1958 National Defense Education Act, to strengthen the national defence by expanding and improving educational programmes

Food and agriculture (1874-1954)

The national concern in the days after the exhausting Civil War was for a continuing and expanding food supply. Food was the central motivation behind the land grants to colleges so that they could develop and disseminate validated agricultural techniques.

The chronological sequence shows this congressional trend:

1862 Morrill Act, land grant to colleges
1874 An Act to encourage the establishment of public marine schools
1887 The Hatch Act for agricultural experimental stations (this was the first federal aid appropriation)
1906 The Dams Act which increased federal money for agricultural experimental stations
1911 The Marine School Act
1914 The Smith-Lever Act to establish co-operative extension work in agriculture and home economics
1925 The Purnell Act, increasing federal money for agricultural experimental stations (also The Capper-Ketchum Act of 1928)
1935 Agricultural Adjustment Act providing for school lunches
1946 Research and Market Act, providing for fishery education and national school-lunch programme
1954 The National School Lunch Act and national school-milk programme

Federal schools and property (1917-53)

Military education, schools and academies were the first, although not the only federally established education institutions. The expansion of the federal government into the financing, construction and programming of schooling has often been linked to construction.

1777 Adoption of plan to begin a military academy
1845 Establishment of US Naval Academy
1917 Smith-Hughes Act establishing federal vocational educational schools
1919 Law to allow federal surplus property available to schools
1920 Smith-Bankhead law providing 37.5 per cent of income from minerals for schools
1933 Civilian Conservation Corps
1935 Works Progress Administration, the creation of the National Youth Administration
1944 The GI Bill, which also distributed surplus property to schools
1946 Mead Act which gave property to schools for veterans
1953 P.L. 815 School Construction
1954 The US Air Force Academy

With the exception of the military academies and the property donations to educational institutions, the most significant venture of the federal government during this earlier era is the Smith-Hughes Act of 1917, which created federal vocational schools. The Depression witnessed the development of education programmes related directly to work and employment: the Civilian Conservation Corps (which operated its own education programmes on site in the federal forests and elsewhere), the National Youth Administration and others. The Smith-Hughes Act established the principle and precedent that the federal government could operate and maintain a specialised school to meet a national need where the local school was unwilling or unable. It was the first categorical grant by the federal government in education, the first grant to be administered by the state education agencies and the first grant whereby the state education agency had to commit matching funds of its own.

Civil and moral rights (1964-)

The 39th Congress which passed the Fourteenth Amendment, also passed the first civil rights act in 1866: 'An Act to protect all persons in the United States in their civil rights, and to furnish the means of their vindication.' Later, the 41st Congress in 1871 extended those civil rights to include also voting rights (the Fifteenth Amendment prohibiting states from denying or abridging voting rights was ratified in 1870), and 'to enforce the rights of citizens of the United States to vote in the several states of the Union'. In the same year, the 41st Congress extended the meaning of these rights to include enforcement procedures against abuse of these rights. That law reads in part:

> That any person who, under color of any law . . . of any State, shall subject, or cause to be subjected, any person within the jurisdiction of the United States to the deprivation of any rights, privileges, or immunities secured by the Constitution of the United States shall . . . be liable to the party injured in any action at law, suit in equity, or other proper proceeding for redress.

There are two noteworthy conditions expressed in this extension of voting and civil rights. The first is the reaffirmation of that phrase originally in the Articles of Confederation, 'privileges and immunities'. The second is that this Act reaffirms the First Amendment privilege of any person 'to petition the government for a redress of grievances'.

The Civil Rights Act of 1964 was long overdue as an expression of national social progress, yet the nation was not prepared for the extensiveness of its provisions. It was sweeping in its provisions and services and specific in what was federal law. The heart of the law was this civil rights entitlement: 'All persons shall be entitled to be free, at any establishment or place, from discrimination or segregation of any kind on the ground of race, color, religion or national origin.' The Civil Rights Act of 1964 in effect nullified all state laws providing for discrimination or segregation. This was the year all schools had *de jure* to end segregation in schooling.

One interesting provision later to be ruled on by the Supreme Court in *Swann vs Charlotte-Mechlenburg* specifically did not empower any official or court of the United States to require 'the transportation of students or pupils from one school to another or one school district to another in order to achieve such racial balance'.

From the assassination of President Kennedy in November 1963, and throughout the Administration of President Johnson, the Congress of the United States was one of the most productive in American history in its emphasis of civil and human needs. In addition to the Civil Rights Act, other major education legislation included:

1963 Vocational Education Act
1965 Elementary and Secondary Education Act
Higher Education Act
International Education Act
1966 National Sea Grant College and Program Act
Child Nutrition Act
National Foundation on the Arts and Humanities
1967 Education Professions Development Act

Consistent with the national evolutionary trend for the federal government to impose and intervene in all domestic concerns in education, we are entering a new phase in civil and moral rights: groups using the schools for promoting certain moral and religious beliefs. Each generation seems to have to face the church/state separation issue in its own way. Recently Congress and the courts have been grappling with prayers in the schools, the banning of books, the content of the curriculum (mostly sex education, but also evolution vs creationism), and income tax relief for parents of children attending parochial schools.

Whereas the Supreme Court will rule on the constitutionality of a schooling controversy, the Congress is responsive as a political forum. Hence, the moral and religious problems of citizens in their schooling districts and counties are heard and acknowledged in the halls and chambers of the national legislature.

The Education for All Handicapped Children Act, popularly known in schooling circles as Public Law 94-142, is a perfect example of the application of the principle of federalism — the partnership of the national and state governments — and the principle of the separation of powers. It was signed into law by President Ford in 1975, and has widened the powers of Congress not only to provide for legislation favourable to a certain categorical group of children, but to specify to local schools how that education shall be conducted.

The deaf, the blind, the orthopaedically impaired, the emotionally disturbed, the mentally ill — all these and others like them were traditionally not admitted to schools, since they were not believed to be 'teachable'. State government often provided institutions to care for the handicapped, but little effort was made to incorporate them into the mainstream of school life. It was not until 1961, when President Kennedy acknowledged publicly that he had a retarded sister and authorised a presidential panel on mental retardation, that the federal government began an active campaign on behalf of the handicapped.

The handicapped were clearly denied equal educational opportunities. Some early programmes were aimed at correcting the handicap rather than teaching the handicapped to live and work usefully in spite of their handicap. Until the 1970s, no one thought much about educating the non-handicapped population about the educational needs of the handicapped.

In 1971 and 1972 two crucial court decisions set the stage for judicial interpretations regarding the education of handicapped children. The Pennsylvania Association for Retarded Children brought suit against the state for failure under the equal protection clause of the Fourteenth Amendment to provide a free public education for all retarded children. The suit charged that the state was denying free access to an education because of children's mental and physical handicaps. A three-judge panel ruled against Pennsylvania, and ordered the state to provide an education to all retarded children between the ages of six and 21 years. It also ordered that this education should be similar to that provided for non-handicapped children. A similar suit, with similar results, occurred in the District of Columbia. This decision then became applicable to all federal jurisdiction. The court, in rendering its decision, based its judgment on the Fifth Amendment due process. As Congress held its oversight hearings in 1973, it had these court decisions to ponder: that all handicapped children, according to provisions in the Fifth and Fourteenth Amendments to the Constitution, were entitled to a free public education.

This particular legislation is especially significant because it compels local schools to provide individualised programmes of educational progress. It is the first instance of education legislation which specifies the nature of the curricular process whether or not the local schools receive financial support from the federal government for handicapped children.

The relation of the national economy to education

Until the Reagan Administration, Congress funded educational programmes in two ways: block grants to states and schools, usually based on defined formulae; and categorical programme grants to states or directly to schools based on proposals competing for discretionary programme funds. Chapter I of the Educational Improvement and Consolidation Act of 1981, for example, combined the convenience of a block grant with a sizeable reduction in the federal work force administering federal programmes and overseeing their maintenance and school compliance. Consolidation, however, is also a way of reducing the amount of appropriated funds.

Political decisions regarding the federal role in education, regardless of their origin, yield here to the fact that money is the controlling factor. Now, more than ever, federal education is more visibly perceived in the context of the functioning economy. Unless and until the economy expands, the federal role in education will be proportionate to the way people perceive other domestic priorities, such as housing and unemployment.

Consequently, the distinction between the two types of grants is not as important in days of uncertain economics as is the amount of money actually appropriated. During the Reagan Administration, for example, based on 1980 fiscal-year levels the amount for education was reduced by 50 per cent throughout 1983. The burden of financing education abruptly shifted to states and localities, which because of their own financial plights, were reluctant to increase state and local tax burdens. Thus, entire local school programmes, some financed through federal funds, were eliminated or substantially reduced.

For example, the Education for Economic Security Act of 1984 delineated the issue in its title. This piece of legislation was Reagan's way of gaining popular and political support for education, while simultaneously consolidating and reducing federal programme support. The various titles of the act were a hotch-potch of previous legislation, including Title V, the Asbestos School Hazard Abatement, for some strange reason included with the promotion of mathematics and science programmes for teachers, presidential awards for teaching excellence and support for schools still undergoing court-ordered desegregation.

However, the primary objective was the support of mathematics and science teachers through the National Science Foundation, not the Department of Education. This was an idea that had emerged from the last years of the Carter Administration, and was adopted by the Reagan team.

The programme used the old formula from the National Defense Education Act of institutes for teachers and stressed the participation of minority populations, now termed 'under-represented and under-served populations'. There were merit scholarships, and a clear 'prohibition against federal control of education'.

At the heart of the legislation was the concept of education for economic security. The means was financial assistance to schools, colleges, state agencies and even private organisations to improve teaching skills in mathematics and science, computer learning and foreign languages. There was nothing new in this enactment except the title: it was if somehow putting it together in this package would thereby spell out the nation's economic health and improvement.

The history of congressional use of consolidated funds for education is not contemporary. As early as 1836, Congress passed a law stipulating the return specifically for schools of surplus revenues. Similarly, in 1891 Congress refunded a direct war tax to the states, three of which used them for school purposes. The Nixon Administration revived the concept of revenue-sharing but without Congressional blessing. When Congress would not grant revenue-sharing for educational programmes, preferring to keep programmes categorically distinct, the Nixon Administration attempted to circumvent Congressional intent by combining programmes administratively.

Despite occasional tensions between the legislative and executive branches of government, there is a strong argument for financial equity in educational opportunity. This has been accentuated recently by court decisions. It is primarily the business of the states to ensure some parity in funding education within its boundaries. Yet the quality of education, as evidenced by national test scores and achievement data, is very uneven and on the decline.

The financial inequalities in education have a long history. A study by the National Education Association in 1926 showed that even then there was a highly diversified pattern of educational opportunities, principally because there were differing state-funding patterns for education. The purpose of the report was to demonstrate that states differ widely in their economic ability to support education. 'Some states', the report noted, 'must bear tax rates five and six times as great as other states to provide a given school opportunity for their children'.

The two major recommendations made by that report were: the establishment of a Department of Education; and the financial equalisation of educational funding. The report stated:

> In recent decades, the question of the proper relation of the federal government to education has been widely discussed and has received much consideration by Congress . . . The first proposal would have the national government develop a program of educational investigation and research through a Department of Education . . . The second proposal would substantially increase federal support of education within the states to achieve greater equality of educational opportunity.

The soundest argument for the federal role in financing education is advanced by Tiedt (1966). A summary of the basic argument for federal aid would include, he states, the equalisation of educational opportunity, the general need for assistance, the national concern for education, the broadening of the tax base, the mobility of the population and the national acceptance of more education for greater numbers.

The most critical argument is financial. It is more cost effective to levy and collect federal money than it is to levy and collect local money. Tiedt explains:

> The cost of levying and collecting $100.00 through federal taxation is $.40, compared to $10.00 as levied and collected by local government agencies. It appears advantageous, therefore, to send tax monies to Washington rather than to local tax collecting agencies.

Yet the arguments against aid to education are equally vocal and strong. They centre around these themes: the impossibility of ever equalising educational opportunity, the threat of federal control in what had been constitutionally accepted local practice, the cost to the taxpayer of federal involvement, the discouragement of local and individual initiative in school affairs, state-wide local opposition felt in the political arena and the infringement of the powers of and opposition from local school boards.

By and large, these are the same arguments against federal involvement in any phase of local or community life, whether the issue is housing, transportation, energy or consumer affairs. Former congressman John Brademas has said:

> Programs of federal aid to elementary and secondary education, the level at which the greatest controversy arises, have simply not been shown to lead to federal control of the curriculum, school teachers, or educational policies. On the contrary, these programs have served not to restrict but to expand the resources, options and effectiveness of local school agencies. The specter of federal domination of the schools through categorical aid has no foundation in fact.

If we can surmise anything from a brief historical analysis of Congress's role in setting educational policy, it is that it has existed from the beginning of the Republic. The federal role in education is thus not a creation of the modern bureaucratic imagination. What does seem to be new is the fear in many communities, on the one hand, of subservience to federal domination and, on the other hand, the tremendous financial, logistic and legal problems experienced by local schools that only the federal government seemed designed to solve.

Congress in 1985, in a desperate attempt to control the enormous $200 billion-plus federal deficit, passed the Gramm-Rudman-Hollings Act which required a balanced budget within six years. It specified automatic budget reductions at intermediate intervals within that six-year period. One part of the law was ruled unconstitutional by a federal court in 1986 because it gave executive powers to the Comptroller General, who administers the General Accounting Office and hence works for Congress. What is pertinent here is that the state of the economy determines federal educational policy.

Regardless of the composition of Congress, the flexibility of the economy, or the overall state of the nation, some congressional legislation for educational programmes, probably consolidated, will always be forthcoming. The reason is disarmingly simple: education is a matter of national security and therefore will always be a subject for national debate and programme development. Yet, if recent trends are any indication, the exact form of the legislative action will be less important than the amount of money appropriated. There is, of course, the perennial debate over how much should go for national defence and how much for domestic and social programmes. Domestically, education can be grouped low among other activities, minimised or disregarded, or receive some acknowledged preference. The degree of funding priority will be conditioned by the relationship Congress has with the President, and the political party in favour in both Houses of Congress and the White House. There will always be a sizeable special-interest group — the teacher lobby is considerable — to ensure that some federal funds for education will merit congressional consideration. Ignoring education can be politically calamitous.

7

People and Policy in
Federal Education Legislation

The Senate of the Republic often abused its authority, defended corrupt officials, waged war ruthlessly, exploited conquered provinces greedily, and suppressed the aspirations of the people for a larger share in the prosperity of Rome. But never elsewhere, except from Trajan to Aurelius, have so much energy, wisdom and skill been applied to statesmanship; and never elsewhere has the idea of service to the state so dominated a government or a people.

Will Durant (1944)

CONGRESS — LAW AS THE EXPRESSION OF PUBLIC OPINION

Is there a revolution under way in the United States and in the Congress? John D. Rockefeller (1973) believes that there is, calling it a 'facilitator of participation'. Jean Francois Revel (1971) describes it as a revolution of dissent: 'The revolution of the twentieth century will take place in the United States. Whether or not that revolution spreads to the rest of the world depends on whether or not it succeeds first in America.' One of the conditions of this revolution of dissent, Revel continues, is a 'critique of management, directed against the waste of material and human resources'. Hubert Humphrey (1968) also spoke of a revolution: 'Equality — or equal freedom for all — is the objective of the never-ending American revolution . . . The first stage in the unfinished American revolution toward human dignity was legislation for civil rights.'

Whether or not these 'revolutions' are descriptive of the same phenomenon or are actual or illusory is immaterial. What is clear is that they are not revolutions of conflict fought with missiles and armour. They are a revolution in social attitudes. They are sudden expressions of a national consciousness, of shifts in the national psyche, of dissent about national policies or the lack of national policies, that usually bring about an adjustment in objectives — and in legislation. Education is a part of that vortex of public expression. Congress, under presidential directive, has diminished the federal role in education. The country has more urgent demands and needs, it now believes.

It follows then, Congress itself is subject to this variable and fluctuating national mood, this revolution of public opinion. This revolution in Congress was brought about by several successive and traumatic events: the convulsions in Vietnam (including the bombing in Cambodia), Watergate, Nixon's resignation and the sudden emergence of the conservative right to power in the White House and in the Senate beginning in 1980. Congress, from the mid-1970s, has institutionalised important changes with laws governing its procedure and behaviour. It has altered significantly its manner of conducting business. The mythology remains, however, and needs to be debunked.

- Younger representatives and Senators rely on committee chairmen and older leaders for advice on how to vote. *False*. With a newly found sense of independence, the Congress as a whole, probably because of the spirit of its younger members, now votes and assumes positions at variance with established party or political bonds. Congressmen are more non-partisan in thinking and action.
- Committee chairmen rise to positions of power based on seniority. *False*. The seniority system still exists but it has weakened considerably. Committee chairmen are now elected by a majority of members in each chamber. As a result, the chairmen are more responsive to their committees.
- Congress crawls with lobbyists who influence legislators more than do the voting constituencies. *Less true than in the past*. On the major issues — like social security and energy — there is too much complexity to yield to a particular lobbying interest. The pressure, consequently, is built in the home district rather than in the congressional corridors. The relative youth of Congress also makes newer members unpredictable. There is no established voting pattern by younger members on certain issues, and so lobbyists cannot easily ascertain voting preferences. Moreover, there are no easy distinctions into conservative/liberal or democratic/republican voting blocs as there once were. The uncertainty of the vote has made the job of the lobbyists more difficult in the absence of defined and predictable voting records.

The exponential rise in congressional business and complexity of the legislation has led to the creation of more subcommittees and with it the expansion of the congressional staff. In 1972 there were

9,402 staff members to serve Congress. Just four years later, in 1976, there were 13,272; by 1980 there were 23,528. Staff competencies and qualifications are high, and staff provide an increasing amount of information and legislative and constituency development to Congress. As Michael Malbin (1980) points out: 'Congress could not function in today's world without the staff on which it has come to depend.'

More staff means more congressional work. In the 1970s the number of committee hearings doubled, roll calls increased five times in the House and ten times in the Senate.

Congress has approximately 250 standing subcommittees. The most powerful members of Congress in the 1950s and 1960s were committee chairs. But by the late 1970s *subcommittee* chairs wielded nearly equal influence, and all chairs found their authority challenged by the new, generally younger breed swept in during the post-Watergate era.

Congress needs to have a constant flow of new ideas to sell to the home, or national, constituency. These 'issues', 'problems' or 'crises' must be able to be legislatively packaged and the staff is under a great deal of pressure to generate these ideas. Sometimes just the suggestion that a member is attempting to get legislation accepted works its magic with the voters back in the district. The proposed drink-driving legislation is one such example that surfaced in 1982. It was a guaranteed national attention-getter and could draw non-partisan votes for passage.

LEGISLATIVE POLICY-MAKING IN EDUCATION

James Madison had acknowledged in *The Federalist Papers* that the legislative authority was more to be feared than the executive. He reiterated this belief while a representative from Virginia on the floor of the House in June, 1787:

> In our government it is, perhaps, less necessary to guard against the abuse of the Executive Department than in any other; because it is not the stronger branch of the system, but the weaker. It therefore must be leveled against the Legislative, for it is the most powerful and most likely to be abused, because it is under the least control.

And again: 'In Republican government the legislative authority necessarily predominates.'

Madison would probably get a hearing today on any legislative floor. In arguing for the first amendments to the Constitution, he feared, even more than the potential abuses of the legislature, the power of the majority over the minority, those powers inherent in the people:

> But I confess that I do conceive, that in a Government modified like this of the United States, the great danger lies rather in the abuse of the community than in the legislative body. The prescriptions in favor of liberty ought to be leveled against that quarter where the greatest danger lies, namely, that which possesses the highest prerogative of power. But this is not found in either the Executive or Legislative departments of government, *but in the body of the people, operating by the majority against the minority.* (emphasis added)

In these arguments to convince his colleagues of the justice and wisdom of amendments protecting individual liberties, later to become the Bill of Rights, Madison feared among other things the tyranny of one religion over another. Would the people, as the supreme holders of the democratic prerogative, abuse their mandate? Or is the national legislature more to be feared today, as Madison suggested, because it holds too much of democracy's trust? I do not believe so. Congress is too attuned to national political pressures, those from the executive and its mercurial responsiveness to the body politic as well as the local constituencies of the representatives.

These political pressures, real or imagined, also play a role in the process of legislating education. For example, regardless of the relative worth and laudable purposes of education legislation — for bilingual education, the handicapped, child-nutrition — there is no guarantee of executive branch administrative effectiveness. The monitoring of funding programmes, called oversight, has generally had a negligible effect on determining overall education policy. Oversight hearings have frequently become verbal abuses of administrators and attacks on Administration policy, especially if it differs from that of the political-party questioning.

During the 1970s educational policy was in the exclusive control of education or education-related committee chairs. Now it is pre-empted by presidential initiative. Jack Shuster observes: 'Congress — itself dominant in federal education policy for the past dozen years — is being eclipsed in importance by the executive branch as the prime mover in this area.' Occasionally, a matter of compelling national attention becomes aligned with education, as did the post-Sputnik National Defense Education Act. This will then override the normal procedures of conducting business about education in Congress. But this is rare.

Congress, when making or amending legislation for education, enters at some point into an established system of action. The methods of arriving at resolution may differ, but there are none the less prescribed approaches: an examination of the historical record and the documentation of precedents; the examination of the content of the proposal; the administrative reorganisation of a programme; finally, political expediency.

The historical record is the simplest congressional approach to formulating education law. The main departures from established precedents in education legislation have been few, although always significant: the land grants under the Northwest Ordinance and the Morrill Act, programmes for returning members of the armed forces (veterans), the Smith-Hughes Act establishing federal schools and strengthening state education agencies, civil rights, and the Elementary and Secondary Education Act, which has no equal in its financial commitment to local schools, or the comprehensiveness of its programme thrust.

The second entry Congress makes into the established stream of education is through the examination of the content of a proposal in a committee whose central task is to reshape and modify the suggested legislation. Public hearings also produce amendments. The primary recommendations are filtered through chairs of related committees — appropriations is one of the most obvious — through committee staff and counsels, and the legislative units of the agencies administering the act.

Congress makes a third entry into the system by prescribing the administrative framework within which the law will be managed, even by designating the names of the offices ('There is established in the Office of Education an Advisory Council on Financial Aid to Students . . . '). Sometimes the whole focus of the legislation can be reorganisation, as is the Department of Education Act, and that establishing the National Institute of Education.

Lastly, political expedience does not always appear obvious to educators, even when an act is passed: the Environmental Education Act serves as a fascinating example.

In the late 1960s, Rep. James Scheuer of New York was going to have to fight for re-election with all his political might. 1968 was the year of re-apportionment, and it was uncertain whether even his private fortune could swing the campaign in his favour. What he heeded was a safe legislative act that would bolster his disappointing record.

The emerging topic of the day was environmental safety. While driving through the streets of New York, Rep. Scheuer had observed broken glass, and wondered about a bill that would help communities clean up the environment, including hauling away abandoned cars. His staff prepared a tentative bill provisionally called the bottle bill. Eventually, elements on school vandalism were included, and by the time draft legislation was prepared on the whole field of environmental education, Scheuer felt the need to have it approved for its legal technicalities. Rather than sending it to the legislative unit in the House providing such service (he had not even read the draft copy), he sent it to Rep. John Brademas's Subcommittee on Select Education. To Scheuer's dismay, Brademas as chairman — also seeking sponsorship for a major piece of legislation, because of uncertainties about his own political future — submitted the bill naming himself as sponsor with Scheuer as co-sponsor.

Whether or not the nation needed or was prepared for it, the educational community received the mixed blessings of this legislation growing out of political survival and necessity.

The Carter Administration, in its 1978 efforts to investigate tax reform while also attempting to help ease inflationary trends by assisting parents of college students with a tuition tax, found itself immediately between Scylla and Charybdis. The proposed recourse was to defer the college tuition tax credit and instead to increase federal scholarships and student loans.

The proposal to Congress was well received, because it temporarily prolonged what tended to be different political decision with its tax credits for the middle class and the predictable backlash from groups excluded. It also served to strengthen the existing loan and scholarship programme with its established constituencies. This included banks, which receive thier interest money while the students are still in college and are guaranteed the principal by government whether the student defaults or not.

In 1978 the Department of HEW reported that a computer check on payrolls revealed that 6,783 federal employees had defaulted on $7.5 million owed to the government in student loans. The total number of defaulters, including those not on government payrolls, was expected to run to 400,000 that year. Why was Congress seeming to agree to the provision of a programme in which the waste of public funds was so high? What kind of oversight would permit this?

Banks received their money, colleges received tuition forms, students got an education, but the government must absorb the cost of defaulters. The US Office of Education had the unhappy image of government collection agency, unless Congress amended the legislation or placed effective controls on its loan policies to students.

Was the student loan programme simply another example of social welfarism in federal education policy: a little something for every congressional district? Or a part of an overall legislative strategy for all federal education? It was neither. It was another example of political expediency at work.

Sometimes political expediency rivets the public attention and divides an already diversive Congress. Forced busing, for example, entered through the backdoor of the appropriations for HEW, a once traditional route for modifying federal education policy. The 1975 anti-busing amendment, whether or not it challenged the Supreme Court in *Swan vs Charlotte-Mechlenburg*, which advocated busing as a means of desegregation, in effect prohibited the executive (in this case HEW) from ordering any student to be bused beyond his neighbourhood school. The Senate, not the House, initiated the debate and passage, another break from the traditional House-dominated education policy amendments.

The supreme irony is that the legislation was meant to mollify constituents of the non-busing advocacy without actually changing policy. Most forced busing was, of course, ordered by the courts and not HEW. Politicians gained tremendously in statute from anti-busing advocacy without changing the status of busing in communities where the courts had already ordered it.

The only way the courts could be prevented from ordering busing where legal practice had already well-established precedents was through an amendment to the Constitution, first proposed in the House and sent to the Judiciary Committee in 1971. The Senate Judiciary Committee actually held hearings on such proposed amendments, but no action has ever been taken. The House Judiciary Committee similarly failed to finalise a constitutional amendment prohibiting busing to achieve desegregation and racial balance.

Political survival, expedience, fear of defeat: these are some of the phrases that identify and characterise much of legislation, including education and its congressional policy formation. The right blend of altruism and the 'national interest' also serve as motivators. Would there have been busing amendments had there not been busing riots and busing rhetoric? The revolution is still at work. The mini-revolution occurs every two years when a new Congress is elected.

Some may be new faces and voices, but all are aware of the need to stand before the electorate for an accounting.

CONGRESSIONAL STAFF

Each committee and subcommittee has an unspecified number of highly qualified professional personnel, including counsellors and lawyers, called 'staffers'. By their individual and collective management of a bill through drafting, hearings, sponsorship, amendments and floor action, and their management of information about the bill, they control its progress, reduce technical disagreements and eliminate political trouble spots. Careful and sound staff work increases its chances of passage.

Staff are responsible for scheduling hearings, calling witnesses and can thus ensure that certain voices are heard or excluded. Staff can control the elements of legislative policy by controlling the content of a hearing.

Michael Malbin (1979) relates an episode during the development of what was then known as The Sunset Bill, introduced by Senator Muskie (later Secretary of State), in an attempt to bring about budget reform in the late 1970s. The episode is an example of how staff control the development of legislation.

> The Ford Administration starts getting into the act at this time as well, offering deals to From [Alvin From, key staff on Muskie's Senate Intergovernmental Relations Subcommittee] that would trade the Administration's support of Sunset for Muskie's support of regulating reform. The offer, which was turned aside, is remarkable less for its content than for the way it was made. Bill Brock, the ranking Republican senator on Government Operation, conveyed the Administration's message not to Muskie but to From, who in turn put it in one of his memos to his boss. According to several Senate aides on other committees this has become standard procedure in the Senate. One former staff director said that at least half of the deals proposed by other senators to his boss were made by the other senators to him.

The staff function has assumed (or been implicitly granted) wide discretionary powers in manipulating legislation, in making deals with other staffers or Congressional representatives or even with the Administration.

Some of the power of the staff can be grasped from Malbin's analysis of this so-called Sunset Bill, whose main provision was the termination of authorisation for most government programmes in order for Congress to get better control over the budgetary process. The staff began the development of this legislative package that would affect the *whole* of government, not just education or one governmental agency, by starting with an idea earlier promulgated by Muskie himself. They then convinced the Senator to let them proceed with draft legislation. They wrote the legislation, did not receive a negative reply from Muskie, rewrote it based on political compromises received from other staffers on other committees, then proceeded to win the consent of outside interest groups. They manoeuvred the draft through the Senate Governmental Affairs Committee, and in general pleaded their case throughout the halls and corridors of congressional power to win passage.

The Sunset Bill never passed, although it was in embryo from 1975 to 1980. Other more pressing national concerns took precedence. Nevertheless, the point here is that congressional staff frequently, without prompting, and with only an implicit blessing to go ahead, take charge of legislation from start to finish. Few members care about the exact details of bills, even the ones they allegedly sponsor; but they always know the political consequences of legislation and how it will affect their political status.

In a related incident, Malbin describes the conference compromise of the 1977 GI Education Bill, in which no member of Congress participated. The joint conference is supposed to be composed of members of both Houses who then work out an agreeable compromise between two differing versions of the same bill. In this case, however, no members were appointed to iron out the differences. It was a 'phantom' conference in which staff reached agreement, and where even new twists appeared that had not appeared in either the House or Senate version of the bill. This new wrinkle, a state matching grant for the cancellation of a federal loan for schooling, eventually became law. Before it was voted on by House and Senate together, no senator or member of Congress have ever seen it, much less debated its merits.

The background was this: the House and Senate had passed, without opposition, two very distinct educational benefits for veterans. The Senate passed its version three weeks before adjournment. Often the timing of bills is itself a political and parliamentary manoeuvre to limit discussion and debate on controversial topics in the bill. The staff was told to come up with a compromise acceptable for joint passage. As Malbin says: 'Key staff people simply sat down for three days in late October and early November and resolved differences between the two bills.'

However, what is alarming is that what the staff agreed to in the negotiating sessions aimed at compromise was not in either version of the bill. Malbin comments: 'Thus, in a single, intense negotiating session, the staff agreed to a "compromise" that in effect was very different from the House bill, the Senate bill, or anything in existing veterans' law.' The bill sailed through with very little debate, and without public explanation of its provisions.

The size of congressional staffs, their delegated and awesome powers to negotiate on behalf of a committee or member and their collective authority have all combined in the last few years to alter substantially the entire way which we look at the legislative process. Congress no longer works as it did in the early 1970s. In fact, its new complexities have been the result partially of the demands made by individuals and groups who seek legislative relief. But it has also grown as a consequence of pressures it has brought upon itself because of its own passage of laws.

Although some staffers may be convincingly independent, they are really fiercely loyal, even deferential, to their bosses. They know the broad policy thinking of the member or committee chair and have some freedom to act within that framework. Senator Claiborne Pell, for example (as Senator Wayne Morse before him), always sought to aid the handicapped and disadvantaged. Staff knew this, and accordingly some legislative language from the Senate on education favoured one or both of those categories and found its way into education enactment.

CONCLUSION

The numerous and profound changes that have been made — electronic voting, open committee hearings, television, the tightening of ethical standards — are less significant than the social changes affecting each new Congress. As Richard Fenno (1985) says: 'It is the members who run Congress . . . We shall get a different kind of Congress when we elect different kinds of congressmen, or when we start applying different standards of judgment to old congressmen.'

The member thinks of and acts first on those ideas and activities that will result in re-election. Re-election means having the best interests of the constituents at heart. The irony is that the personal interests of the political leader become consonant with the larger interests of the community.

But the real paradox is that the rhetoric of re-election, true of presidents as well as representatives, is against the institution of Congress, or against 'Washington'. Politicians get elected or re-elected based on the intensity of their anti-government campaign.

Finally, we will get legislation passed by Congress for general and specific education categories, for the benefit of individuals as well as institutions, not only because it is a long, well-established tradition, but because we consistently elect members to Congress who support the belief that congressional legislation for education is both necessary and desirable for the national good.

Some, like Alvin Toffler (1970), suggest that Congress itself needs drastic revision:

> The Congress is so overloaded by conflicting demands and oceans of unsynthesized data, so many pressures and demands for instant response. The institution is creaking and overloaded and unable to churn out intelligent decisions. Government policymakers are unable to make high priority decisions, or making them badly, while they make thousands of small decisions. When a major problem arises, the solution is usually too late and seldom produces the desired impact.

Congress must sometimes wait on the slow, often imperceptible formation of a national consensus: the build-up of a collective expression. Vietnam was one, then Watergate, energy, the growth of government itself. Assessing the people's mood, testing the political climate, is not only a measure of a politician's or legislator's endurance in office. It is also a test of that national feeling. For to outrun the populace, or worse, to think *for* them, is eventually to render the leader powerless. Woodrow Wilson was one such, Adlai Stevenson another, and Richard Nixon a third. New social relationships, not new political theories, are what bind the law-makers and the law-abiders.

One of the most distinguishing features of the Congress, and indeed American democracy as noted earlier, is *representative* democracy. What is certain is that representative government no longer fits the textbook model. The modern legislator is not merely called upon to assent to executive judgement (as was hastily done in the Gulf of Tonkin Resolution) but to counter it, as was done under Richard Nixon; not to consent to making laws but to initiate them. As we have seen, whatever our particular views on federal education legislation, when new education legislation emanates from Congress, the imprint of the congressional staff will be on it.

But the legislature is not alone in the authority of the law. It may *will* the law, but it cannot execute it. The working partnership on policy in education of executive and legislative constitutes the essence of representative democratic government. Without administration, the law would fail. Without laws, the administration fails. The singular importance of this inter-governmental relationship, and this constitutional and indispensible part of democratic government, is the subject of Part IV of this book.

Part Four: The Federal Executive and Education

It is easy to perceive that the American democracy frequently errs in the choice of the individuals to whom it entrusts the power of the administration; but it is more difficult to say why the State prospers under their rule.

Alexis de Tocqueville
Democracy in America

8

Presidential Statements on Education

The people who daily rush by the ornate columned building at 26 Wall Street in New York City have little idea of its significance, according to the National Park Service rangers who are its caretakers. The rangers themselves, with their Smokey Bear hats, symbol of the great environmental vistas in the west, seem out of place in the cluster of towering financial institutions.

But the rangers are not building guards. They are the custodians of a precious national treasure: the site where representative national government and democracy began.

The original building was torn down in 1812, at the time of the second war with the British. In 1735 John Peter Zanger went on trial for championing the freedom of the press. The Stamp Act Congress convened there in 1765. The Second Continental Congress met there in 1785. The building was the site of the first Capitol of the United States, where Congress first met, where the Bill of Rights was adopted and where the US Supreme Court was established. Probably no building outside the present US Capitol building is as important in United States history. Here too George Washington was sworn in as the first American President. His inauguration began the history of presidential statements on education.

According to Article II of the Constitution:

The executive power shall be vested in a President of the United States of America . . . He shall from time to time give to the Congress information of the state of the Union, and recommend to their consideration such measures as he shall judge necessary and expedient. [Furthermore] he shall also take care that the laws be faithfully executed.

The powers constitutionally delegated to the executive are thus: to give information to Congress; to recommend legislation to Congress; and to uphold the laws that Congress has passed and the president has signed. This constitutional definition is perhaps deliberately ambiguous; it is certainly not operationally exact in the world of political realism. There is, however, no doubting that the educational thinking of the president on policy matters does become known throughout the federal bureaucracy.

The practical educational policies can be as distinctive as in the forceful trend-setting Johnson era, the special revenue-sharing of the Nixon years, the tax credit relief of the Carter Administration, or the reduction in all domestic federal spending of the Reagan Administration.

The art of dealing with Congress on an equal footing was new for George Washington and there were no precedents to guide him. On the one occasion when he decided to go with an Indian treaty to Congress for their 'advice', he was rebuffed, ostensibly so that the Congress might deliberate longer on the subject. He never went to either chamber again. Alexander Hamilton and Thomas Jefferson, however, as Washington's cabinet officers during that first Administration had no such reluctance toward the legislative branch, and went often to the Hill to influence law-makers. The Ways and Means Committee in the House was probably created specifically to resist Hamilton's pervasive influence in fiscal proceedings.

In the nineteenth century no president dominated Congress, but Theodore Roosevelt introduced a novel concept that radically revised presidential relations with Congress. The 'Square Deal' was simply Roosevelt's entire legislative programme. Speaker of the House Cannon repelled it, but Woodrow Wilson in 1913 lobbied for his programme, the 'New Freedom', in the congressional committee rooms. Scholar, university president, political scientist turned politician, Wilson became in effect the chief legislator for the nation, much as the British prime minister was to Parliament. It was a political model with which he identified. Compared with Franklin Roosevelt's 'New Deal' and Truman's 'Fair Deal' these early presidential thrusts into the law-making process seem child's play.

Eisenhower was the first to introduce a White House assistant, Bryce Harlow, as chief lobbyist for the Administration. But John Kennedy became his own lobbyist, although he delegated tremendous power to Larry O'Brien, who had the authority to accept or reject legislative substance. What presidents say, either on their own account or through intermediaries, has influenced federal educational policy in this century as the presidency itself expanded in power and persuasion.

Presidential statements, whether on education or any matter incumbent upon the executive, vary not only in context but in form of presentation. The most formal is the 'State of the Union address', because that is the phrase prescribed by the Constitution for presidential reporting to Congress. But messages and requests for congressional legislative action are also a part of the executive's constitutional obligation: 'He shall from time to time give to the Congress information of the state of the Union, and recommend to their consideration such measures as he shall judge necessary and expedient.'

The period from 1861 to 1913, from the Administration of President Lincoln to President Wilson, was a formative one in American federal executive policy toward education. It contained the seeds of many present legislative education programmes. It was a time when the majority of presidents, especially Grant, Hayes and Arthur, valiantly attempted to persuade an indifferent Congress to pass an education bill. They were not successful, and except for Lincoln's victory in the Morrill Act, there was in this period no education legislation at all.

State of the Union addresses have been the most widely used means of synthesising presidential thought and communicating it to the Congress. From 1809 to 1913, through the 25 presidencies from Madison to Wilson, most State of the Union addresses were no more than summaries of cabinet reports to the president. The president simply passed on his report of what the total government was doing.

There were a few, notably Jackson, Lincoln and Theodore Roosevelt, who departed from the standard set by others to appeal directly to the public through congressional messages. Often the president did not even deliver the address. Jefferson decided not to go personally to Congress to make his State of the Union address as Washington and Adams had. President Wilson, over 100 years later, resurrected the tradition of personal delivery before the assembled Congress to take advantage of wider press coverage. Calvin Coolidge did not go to Congress. Franklin D. Roosevelt did, and it is unlikely the tradition will ever again revert to a mere written communication.

From Lincoln to Wilson, with the sole exception of the separated two terms of President Grover Cleveland, all the Administrations were Republican. This was a time in American history that witnessed the painful reconstruction of a shattered economy and a disenfranchised people and a gradual adjustment to an industrialised age. It also marked an era which confronted the twentieth century and mechanised warfare. Nevertheless, there was throughout repeated appeals from Republican presidents for the passage of some kind of financial aid bill for education.

THE 1860s

If James Buchanan, the fifteenth president of the United States, vetoed the first Morrill Bill establishing land-grant colleges in 1859, it was because he believed a constitutional amendment was needed before the federal government could provide assistance for education. He felt that such an action without the amendment violated states' rights. President Lincoln had no such reservations about the federal prerogative and signed the Morrill Act into law in July 1862.

The law established forever the land-grant colleges and prescribed the curriculum:

> To the endowment, support, and maintenance of at least one college where the leading object shall be, without excluding other scientific and classical studies and including military tactics, to teach such branches of learning as are related to agriculture and the mechanic arts.

Andrew Johnson's one term was a difficult one for the nation: it had to come to terms with the assassination of a former president and Johnson's impeachment. However, as Governor of Tennessee, Johnson had early in his political career emphasised education. His remarks at the Tennessee State Agricultural Fair in 1857 reveal his thinking on what within five years would become the most significant higher education legislation of the century, the Morrill Act creating the land-grant colleges:

> It is high time the agriculturists and mechanics of our country had commenced educating their children . . . so as to make labor respectable . . . these leading interests might come to be efficiently represented in every department of the government.

Johnson's Biennial Message to the Tennessee State Legislature in Nashville on 19 December 1853 while he was Governor, had resulted in the biggest educational advancement in the history of Tennessee, a state law which provided for a state tax to support public schools:

All very readily concur in the opinion that something ought to be done to promote the cause of education, and still there are no effective steps taken . . . If we are sincere in what we profess for the cause of education, we should, without hesitation, provide means to accomplish it. There is one way, if *no* other, that the children of the State can be educated, which is obvious to all, and that is, to levy and collect a tax from the people of the whole State.

Had the nation not been engaged in internal reconstruction one wonders what President Andrew Johnson might have accomplished on behalf of education during his presidential Administration.

URGING AN EDUCATION ACT: GRANT, HAYES AND ARTHUR

It was President Grant who reported to the Congress in 1870 on the establishment of a Bureau of Education. Grant was also the first president to request a university in the District of Columbia, although Washington, Jefferson and Madison had urged a 'national university' to be located in the federal district. Perhaps most significantly, Grant advocated a constitutional amendment guaranteeing equal education for all. The education of the Negro and the eradication of illiteracy were the two most pressing educational issues of the 1870s.

Grant strongly endorsed a bill to provide a fund for education from the sale of public lands. The House during the 41st Congress had passed such a bill in 1872, by a majority of 19. Even with Grant's endorsement, however, it failed in the Senate. Again in 1875 he urged that 'the education of the masses becomes the first necessity for the preservation of our institutions'. He wanted his recommended constitutional amendment to require states to provide free schools. Scores of bills were introduced during his Administration but none ever passed Congress. Grant dropped the pursuit of his educational act from his annual message to Congress in 1876 after an educational bill was defeated by an overwhelming vote. Clearly, federal aid to education had not yet come of age.

Grant's successor, President Hayes, also urged congressional legislation for education. He spoke of the adoption of an education act in each of his three annual messages to Congress. 'No more fundamental responsibility rests upon Congress than that of devising appropriate measures of financial aid to education, supplemental to local action in the States,' he said in his third annual message. President Garfield too took up the banner for education, after Hayes was unable to coax Congress into adopting an educational act. His assassination postponed proposals in support of national education.

President Arthur, although more reserved in his advancement of education, suggested that federal funds could be 'wisely distributed in the different states according to the ratio of illiteracy', an intriguing concept. He too promoted education in all three of his annual messages. The Senate defeated one measure, after protracted debate, in February 1883, by the close vote of 82 to 80. President Arthur's third message to Congress had been an encouragement to consider 'whether some federal aid should not be extended to public elementary education wherever adequate provision thereof has not already been made'. This time the Senate did pass a resolution, but the House failed to take any action and nothing ever resulted.

President Arthur's requests to Congress for federal education funds to reduce illiteracy and to assist elementary schools 'whenever adequate provision has not already been made' were provocative and innovative for the 1880s. His concern about illiteracy today finds expression in federal aid distributed according to a poverty ratio of the parents of school-aged children. The objective of such Acts as the former Title I of The Elementary and Secondary Education Act of 1964 is the same that Arthur envisaged: to increase school achievement among those children who need it most, the sons and daughters of parents who have themselves been low achievers in school.

President Cleveland, whose eight years — two separated terms — were the only ones of the Democratic Party in the 52 years of Republican denomination of the White House, showed little interest in education. A few education bills were introduced, and one passed the Senate in 1886. But the House again failed to take any action.

Benjamin Harrison, who was president after Cleveland's first term, did indeed help to usher in new bills for federal aid to schools in Congress, but again none ever emerged from the House Committee on Education and Labor.

Sometimes more can be revealed in personal letters, memorabilia and jottings than in official correspondence. A quote from President Theodore Roosevelt's letters to the oldest of his four boys demonstrates his high regard for education. It is dated 'The White House, 1903':

> I wonder whether there can come in life a thrill of greater exaltation and rapture than that which comes to one between the ages of say six and fourteen, when the library door is thrown open and you walk in to see all the gifts, like a materialized fairy land, arrayed on your special table. (Bishop, 1919)

THE FIRST STIRRINGS: WILSON TO FRANKLIN ROOSEVELT

Woodrow Wilson (1889) observed:

> Our modern systems of public education are more thorough than the ancient, notwithstanding the fact that we regard the individual as something other than a mere servant of the state, and educate him first of all for himself.

The Administration of President Wilson was a time notable for the expansion of co-operative federalism, not the stiff, dual federalism which recognised the state and the federal government as equally sovereign. Federal aid progammes grew not only for teaching materials for the blind, but for aid for veterans and agricultural experimental stations through land-grant colleges. President Wilson also accelerated the development of vocational education and vocational rehabilitation programmes.

Presidents Harding, Coolidge and Hoover were unimpressed with the arguments or the data about the educational inequalities in state and local school systems. They simply did not believe that education was in any way the responsibility of the federal government. But they were the first presidents in the history of the republic to express such thinking. One can say that these contemporary presidents introduced the novel idea that the federal government should not participate in education in any way. Some presidents, like Cleveland, were indifferent. But no president before this century had made the lack of federal involvement in education a policy matter.

Herbert Hoover was perhaps the first president to feel the pressure of an education lobby. He also appointed a committee to investigate education and the federal role, developed a nation-wide programme to eradicate illiteracy by means of adult education, and recommended an Assistant Secretary in the Department of Interior where the Bureau of Education was then located. In his memoirs Hoover (1952) wrote:

> Certain very vocal education associations were constantly demanding Federal support to the whole school system of the nation. I was not opposed to Federal aid to backward areas where there was genuine need. But this was not the objective of the demands. The associations wanted the Federal head under every state and county tent.

Hoover doubted that 'thinking educators' really wanted a Department of Education — a National Education Association recommendation from a study in 1926 — or direct subsidies from the federal government to schools. So, to circumvent the political lobbying pressure, Hoover appointed a committee in June 1929, his first year in office, to study the matter and report back to him. The committee's report was unanimous: 'The Federal government should not encroach upon the public school systems.'

The Hoover Administration's programme for abolishing illiteracy was in effect a voluntary organisational effort. The informal organisation used was adult education. The programme helped establish such activities in 43 states, and state authorities and civic organisations helped set up adult education classes. Hoover claimed that the Democratic majority in Congress kept him from appointing an Assistant Secretary for Education. It is an historical fact that Congress did not vote for the measure.

The most significant educational accomplishment of the immediate post-World War II years was the passage of the GI Bill of Rights. This veterans' measure included massive funds for educational benefits. Franklin D. Roosevelt had appointed a committee of educators in 1942 to study and develop a programme for the training and education of veterans, and within one year Roosevelt's recommendations were ready for Congress. They included federal aid for veterans to study up to one year, and for certain ex-servicemen and women up to three years for 'specialized, technical or professional education'.

The war itself had a disrupting influence on all education during the Roosevelt Administration. Colleges stood idle when students and teachers alike were drafted or volunteered. For higher education institutions, Roosevelt proposed using college facilities for training and mobilisation purposes. Five hundred colleges became the training ground for 300,000 soldiers.

The National Science Foundation arose from Roosevelt's request for post-war recovery and the Administration's emphasis on scientific research and development. Roosevelt's encouragement of government and university co-operation in government-sponsored investigations in science and technology brought about social disruption on campuses over 20 years later when social activists condemned colleges and universities for accepting federal funds for the development of war materials.

Roosevelt's request for government subsidies for colleges and universities served to strengthen even liberal arts institutions into centres for vocational education and government research. What

Roosevelt had intended as a temporary post-war relief measure for colleges became a permanent educational fixture. His was one of the country's most intellectually stimulating Administrations and a point of high adventure in government activity even for education.

President Franklin D. Roosevelt's State of the Union message on 6 January 1945 spelled out a new programme for an economic bill of rights. Near the end of the message, he promised to send to Congress a special message on education and related topics. He died before it could be developed.

BREAKTHROUGHS: TRUMAN AND EISENHOWER

President Harry S. Truman, despite his preoccupation with the aftermath of World War II and the military activities of the Korean War, was an exceptionally vigorous champion of federal educational aid. His first annual message to Congress is perhaps the strongest on federal assistance in education ever sent by a president to Congress. I quote substantial sections of that message to demonstrate the importance of its impact in 1946:

- Although the major responsibility for financing education rests with the States, some assistance has long been given by the Federal government. Further assistance is desirable and essential.
- It is essential to provide adequate elementary and secondary schools everywhere and additional educational opportunities for large numbers of people beyond the secondary school level.
- It is essential for the Federal Government to provide financial aid to assist the States in assuring more nearly equal opportunities for a good education.
- Higher incomes should make it possible for State and local governments and for individuals to support higher and more adequate expenditures for education. But inequality among the States will still remain, and Federal help will still be needed.
- The Federal Government has not sought, and will not seek, to dominate education in the States. It should continue its historic role of leadership and advice and, for the purpose of equalizing educational opportunity, it should extend further financial support to the cause of education in areas where this is desirable.

Except for specific categorical requests, it is all there: Federal aid (not domination), the equalising of educational opportunity, school construction and facilities, tax relief through federal educational aid, post-secondary education assistance, state education assistance, relief to equalise educational inequalities between states, state and local matching grants.

Although these ideas did not find favour with the succeeding Administration of President Eisenhower, they contain the substance of later federal involvement in education.

The Republican Administration of President Dwight Eisenhower, former college president, showed little interest in federal education assistance. Had it not been for the seeming technological superiority of Russian earth-orbiting satellites, federal education programmes would never have received such an enthusiastic endorsement from a president uncommitted to promoting them. The year was 1958.

The National Defense Education Act — 'to strengthen the national defense and to encourage and assist in the expansion and improvement of educational programs to meet critical national needs' — elevated Eisenhower as an educational advocate. It could not help but improve his image in the minds of educators who saw him as a roadblock to the Supreme Court's *Brown* decision four years earlier. Fittingly, for a war hero turned president, the formal language of the National Defense Education Act was designed to appeal to a public tempered by World War II. However, its practical effect was to energise the entire educational system. The sudden jolt of federal expansion with the accompaniment of funding changed forever the static relationship between schools and colleges and the federal government. The complacency of the 1950s was shattered and the inertia of the schooling process had begun to crumble. Educational practice would no longer go unchallenged. And among the first questions was this: 'Why can Johnny not read?'

THE INCOMPARABLE 1960s: KENNEDY AND JOHNSON

Both Democrat and Republican national conventions in the summer of 1960 sported education planks which set out to appeal to education-block voters. The education plank of the Democrats in their national convention in Los Angeles on 12 July 1960, read:

> We believe that America can best meet its educational obligations only with generous financial support, within the traditional framework of local control. The assistance will take the form of federal grants to states for educational purposes they deem most

pressing, including classroom construction and teachers' salaries.

It was post-Sputnik, it was post-war, baby-boom time, and the convention nominated John Kennedy. The Republican convention began in Chicago on 27 July 1960. It nominated Richard Nixon and its education plank read:

> The federal government should assist selectively in strengthening education without interfering with full local control of schools. One objective of such federal assistance should be to help equalize educational opportunities.

There followed recommendations for school construction, vocational education, libraries, basic research, special education, college housing, student loans, tax laws to offset tuition costs and the like. The mood of educational generosity coupled with the Russian spy-in-the-sky satellites, and the attendant hysteria and threat to national security, was evident in both planks.

In the waning days of the Eisenhower Administration a Senate amendment had been introduced for federal funds for school construction and teacher salaries. In 1959 Senator, and presidential candidate-to-be, Richard Nixon had cast the deciding vote against that amendment. However, after his narrow election win in 1960, Kennedy soon submitted an education message. It was entitled simply, 'Message from the President of the United States Relative to American Education'. It was submitted to Congress on 20 February 1961 (appropriately Washington's birthday). He said in that message: 'I recommend to the Congress a three-year program of general Federal assistance for public elementary and secondary classroom construction and teachers' salaries.'

It was a bold manoeuvre, but bound to fail even in a democratically controlled Congress because it tampered with the salaries of teachers, traditionally a local school's rights. In fact, the 1965 White House Conference on Education was later to oppose 'any federal control over educational use of funds in local districts'. It also did not resolve the issue of public aid to parochial schools.

The debates that reverberated in Congress during the 1960s over the extent of federal control had simply not been allowed to surface through preceding administrations. But the old arguments and cliches were there and the public was confused. People sought, on the one hand, the protection of their schools from the alleged domination of big government and, on the other hand, a counter-thrust to Russian

131

satellite superiority.

The National Education Association testimony before the Subcommittee on Education in 1961 tried to soothe the fears of federal control: 'Some people believe there is something inherently wrong using Federal money for education. Why? Federal money is used for practically every other purpose.'

Abraham Ribicoff, then President Kennedy's Secretary of the Department of HEW gave testimony on Kennedy's School Assistance Act before the Senate Subcommittee on Labor and Public Welfare in 1961: 'The Federal role has been a legitimate and accepted part of American Educational experience since the founding of the Republic. For 175 years, Federal aid to education has helped to serve the national interest.'

President Kennedy's Administration, charismatic and promising in 1960, was marred by Kennedy's own cautious and pragmatic approach to politics, especially social issues. His fierce competitive political spirit would not allow him to consider the possibility of failure. Consequently, early in his Administration he did not recommend legislation to Congress that might not pass. He had won the presidency on the narrowest of electoral margins. He did not have the persuasive skills that Lyndon Johnson would bring to that office.

Clearly, the most significant domestic issue of the day was civil rights. Blacks could neither vote nor attend white schools. James Meredith's attempts to enter the University of Mississippi was the focal point of the quest for civil equality.

When Kennedy ordered the army troops in at Oxford, Mississippi, his hand was forced as commander in chief and his caution ended. Yet he was still hesitant about advancing the cause of civil rights in schooling. He feared losing the South's political support in the 1964 election campaign.

Nevertheless, Kennedy was the first American president to place the question of civil rights before the American public and make it a moral issue. In doing so, he lost the South, and his pending legislation was stalled in Congress. Sadly, however, he declined to take part in the Washington, DC demonstration, which became the largest peaceful demonstration in the history of America, and one which changed the course of civil rights forever in America.

It is not so much the sum or substance of what his Administration was or stood for, as what he himself brought to government: a forceful optimism for what government could do, a sense of hope in national life America has never recaptured. His principal monument in Washington, DC is not a statue or obelisk. It is a Center for the

Performing Arts.

Lyndon Johnson's Elementary and Secondary Education Act (ESEA) was signed after only 87 days in Congress. Although the church/state issue did arise once in the House hearings, it was effectively suppressed and there was no amendment submitted by the House. The Senate passed on the measure without changing even a comma. It was the first ever billion-dollar bill for education and one of the largest in the history of government.

President Johnson recalled the occasion:

> I will never do anything in my entire life, now or in the future, that excites me more, or benefits the nation I serve more, or makes the land and all the people better and wiser and stronger, or anything that I think means more to freedom and justice in the world than what we have done with this education bill . . . This is the most important bill I will ever sign.

Johnson's hero annd mentor was Franklin D. Roosevelt, than whom no man in the history of American politics and the presidency had used government more adroitly to social advantage. LBJ admired FDR tremendously, and in 1935 after a stint working as aide for a Texas congressman, went back to Texas as the state director of the National Youth Administration, one of FDR's foremost social programmes with a strong education and training component. In his memoirs, Johnson (1971) describes the educational situation while he was president:

> By the 1960s the public schools were in a state of crisis beset by problems that had been multiplying since World War II. School enrolments had increased 43 per cent in one decade. Classrooms were overcrowded. Teaching staffs were undermanned and underpaid. The quality of instruction had declined . . . It was obvious that federal aid was urgently needed to avert disaster.

There was no hesitation about Johnson's use of the federal government to help solve a national problem. He continues: 'I made a personal decision during the 1964 Presidential campaign to make education a fundamental issue and to put it high on the nation's agenda.'

There is no doubt that the culmination of the electoral mandate and education pledge resulted in the ESEA: 'The bill was placed in the highest priority category. I resolved to put the entire power and prestige of the Presidency behind it.'

There was, of course, other education legislation that would follow:

the Higher Education Act, Teacher Corps, the Educational Opportunity Act, the Adult Education Act. 'Altogether we passed sixty education bills,' Johnson notes. But ESEA was the brightest star in the firmament: 'To my mind, the outstanding significance of the ESEA was that it established a foundation on which the country could work toward educational achievement, with equal quality and opportunity for the future.' He remembered the long history of presidential statement and congressional inaction: 'Since 1870, almost a hundred years ago, we have been trying to do what we have just done — pass an elementary school bill for all the children of America.'

With the stroke of the presidential pen, Johnson resolved education issues that had long dead-locked the Congress: the relation of parochial and private (church) schools to public schools in general aid; the issue of general aid to segregated schools (the Civil Rights Act in 1964 had eliminated that problem) and the prescription of categorical aid to students not schools, specifically the disadvantaged student: 'During the five years of my Presidency annual investments in progams increased . . . for education from $2.3 billion to $10.8 billion.' It would be a tough, if not impossible act to follow.

POLICY SHIFTS: NIXON TO REAGAN

The Nixon Administration, despite the active and occasionally imaginative proposals advanced particularly in the field of higher education by Daniel Moynihan, is not usually associated with a vigorous educational commitment. Prior to election as president, Richard Nixon had not placed any entries in his career record that identified him in any way with education. Like other preceding Administrations, war, the economy, and the increasing alienation and the demonstrable oppositon of students pre-empted executive energies.

The year 1970 was not one of outstanding educational achievements. In January President Nixon vetoed the Labor, HEW and OEO appropriations bill. The president wanted reform in education without more federal dollars. In February he fired Leon Panetta (later congressman from California) the Director of the Office of Civil Rights on the grounds of excessive zeal in carrying out desegregation laws. In April he reluctantly signed the elementary and secondary education amendments. Vice-President Agnew's purple prose speeches called for the expulsion of protesting students; and on 30 April Nixon announced that troops were being sent into Cambodia. In May four students were shot at Kent State; Secretary of the

Interior Walter Hickel made public his letter to Nixon in which he protested against the Administration's policies towards the young: 75,000 demonstrators marched on Washington; two students were killed by police at Jackson State. On 10 June US Education Commissioner James Allen was fired for his public disagreement with the war and desegregation policies.

In March 1970 the twin messages on education reform and higher education had been sent to Congress. It was not propitious timing. Neither was Nixon's second veto of the education appropriation the following August. The gulf between the Administration and the education community appeared insuperable.

It has been commonly believed that Nixon's development of education proposals was politically motivated to assuage the democratically controlled Congress and to pacify the educational community. I believe, however, that although President Nixon did not spend inordinate energies on education (few presidents do) the special education messages to Congress in March 1970 stand out as compelling documents. They embody the best of social science research about education and contain purposeful structural and conceptual points of departure.

The structural proposals — The National Institute of Education and the President's Commission on School Finance — became operational. The National Foundation for Higher Education, Moynihan's planned creation of a separate agency for higher education programmes, did not materialise. However, the Fund for the Improvement of Post-Secondary Education became the congressional compromise.

Conceptually, both messages contained innovative and occasionally daring proposals. Consider a few of them: the encouragement of broader, more sensitive measuring instruments for educational achievement; endorsement of the Right to Read and the Experimental Schools programmes; an emphasis on educational television as an aid to learning; a focus on early childhood learning ('the First Five Years of Life'); career education (originally intended only for community colleges); the challenge of educational reform throughout the total system.

These recommendations were extraordinary, not only because they came directly from the president but because of their breadth and scope. To be sure, there were some of the standard educational platitudes and a few of the speech writer's catchphrases ('child's play is serious business'). But the substance of both messages is unquestionably progressive and detailed.

Eventually, the war, student and public protestations against it, the sliding economy and, of course, Watergate, brought the presidency to an uncommon low-point in American history. Perhaps it was cyclic or inevitable. But the logic and argumentation of Nixon's twin education messages, lost as they were in the controversy about the man himself, still represent some of the best federal educational policy ever to emerge from the executive and the White House.

In 1971, with a new Secretary of HEW, Eliott Richardson, and a new Commissioner of Education, Sidney Marland, three more education messages were sent to Congress. Moynihan had departed for Harvard, and there was no one of any stature or political muscle in the White House to challenge the modifications of the original education messages Nixon submitted in March 1970. Henceforward, Richardson and Marland dominated education policy largely because the White House had ignored education development after 1970. As Chester Finn (1977) observes: 'The White House may unwittingly have improved the prospects for its education program by abandoning interest in it. This presidential neglect of education policy allowed others in the administration to fill the vacuum.' The federal executive, as embodied by the president, had lost the time, the momentum and the spirit of the original team that put together the education messages. President Gerald Ford did not recover it.

President Jimmy Carter's first education message to Congress in February 1978 urged the creation of a Department of Education, a campaign promise. Besides that organisational change, the message proposed changes in existing federal education statutes including, notably: a commitment to basic skills, a re-targeting of Emergency School Aid Act monies to help schools through the desegregation transition, a revision of the Impact Aid formula, a strengthening of bilingual education, and a request to have private school students participate in federally funded education programmes.

A controversial feature was college student assistance. Carter proposed a major expansion of student aid programmes for college students. The Administration proposed increasing from three million to five million the number of participating students. It opposed the tuition tax credit which was finding favour in the Congress.

The special education message was designed to maintain friends and alliances without antagonising anyone in the establishment. The President promised:

> We must give education a more prominent and visible role in the federal government. This budget reflects the judgment, widely shared by the Congress, that improving the education of our

children is a wise investment in our future.

The Carter Administration was pledged to carry out the tradition of the strong elementary and secondary education programme begun during the Johnson Administration:

> Since the Administration of Lyndon Johnson the primary role of these Federal programs [in elementary and secondary education] has been to support improvements in educational opportunities and achievement . . . I propose to continue and strengthen the use of Federal resources to meet special needs.

On 31 July 1981 Congress passed an historic bill reducing a $35.3 billion-dollar governmental package in the federal budget. The legislative measure repealed outright scores of social and educational programmes long considered sacred to their constituencies and special-interest groups. For a half century they had been a part of federal and social life. But the Reagan Administration's trend was clear and unmistakable: power was not to be located in Washington, DC.

This sweeping budget cut was achieved early by the Reagan Administration, alienating both bureaucrats and the interest-group members. It was the end of a complex network of social action programmes begun under the New Deal, and constituted the most monumental turnaround in federal policy in this century. Over 250 programmes were consolidated or reduced. And this was accomplished without congressional hearings, testimony or debate. The policy was implemented by a little-known review process known as *reconciliation*.

The reconciliation process was never used with such incisiveness. Previously, reconciliation was a vehicle for resolving the failure to achieve a compromise after exhausting other budget procedures at the end of the budget-review process. Through the Office of Management and Budget, Reagan used it at the beginning of the budget-review process. Few programmes met the Reagan Administration's criteria for acceptance.

Republicans were jubilant at this budgetary victory. Senator Howard Baker of Tennessee made these comments in the Senate:

> The alleged impossible conference has produced one of the most impressive and monumental legislative accomplishments of this century. It has been . . . a most powerful vehicle for abating the

limitless expenditures of the past . . . the conference will report savings for the next fiscal year in the range of $35 billion, and provide for an additional $130 billion plus over the next three years through reductions in Federal programs.

Reagan's novel governmental thrust brought a new consciousness to the American public. It was no longer the lopping off of a few programmes here, and the reducing of dollars there. It was the alteration of the course of government itself. President Reagan termed the tax bill and the budget-cutting bill, the first in his Administration, 'another great revolution and experiment' in federalism, a plan to return federal authority to the States: 'With our economic proposals we are staging a quiet federalist revolution. It is a revolution that promises to be one of the most exciting and noteworthy in our generation.' What appeared to be merely a form of cost-benefit during economically difficult times, was a radical redefinition of government itself. The new philosophy was outlined in the *Budget Revisions* for 1982 of the Office of Management and Budget:

> Education policy has historically been the prerogative of State and local communities. In recent years the Federal government has become increasingly involved in this non-Federal responsibility. The Administration proposes to shift control over education policy from the Federal government to State and local authorities through the consolidation of forty-four elementary and secondary education grant programs into two block grants.

On the contrary, however, as this study shows, the federal role in education has been a continuous partnership, an extension of democratic governance and an illustration of national government in the domestic life of the people. Local control of education and even absolute state control are myths. The federal involvement in education dates from the earliest days of independence, prior even to the establishment of most states, and certainly prior to the development of the common school and its traditions.

Yet until this century no president had even suggested that there should be an absence of federal participation in education. By 1983, at the end of his first term in office, Reagan had isolated the Department of Education from policy initiative and had used his unique communicative skills to foster and promote his own package of education ideas, including merit pay for teachers, tuition tax credits and educational vouchers. He also proposed a constitutional amendment allowing prayers in public schools.

9

Presidential Policy Formation
in Education

The executive power shall be vested in a President.
                                    The Constitution: Article II

Executive education policy, like any other government policy, always
emanates from the president himself. This is true regardless of the
government agency or function assigned to plan or evaluate governmental priorities.

The president can make known his education policy preferences
in several ways. At least five methods have been used by presidents:

- Committees and Commissions (including task forces)
- Presidential Appointments
- Agencies
- Messages to Congress
- Appeals to the Public: the White House Conferences

Analysis of each of these presidential procedures will illustrate how
presidents act when they make a decision to use the federal government on behalf of education.

COMMITTEES AND COMMISSIONS

A committee or commission can be used by a president to recommend acceptable policy for legislation. Alternatively, he can use it
to dissipate an idea or plan for education into meaningless activity.

The Hovde Report under President Kennedy and the Gardner
Report under President Johnson are examples of presidential task
forces whose recommendations were adopted. The Pifer Report under
President Nixon is an example of an education task force whose suggestions were never meant to be accepted. Nixon actually rejected
the recommendations of the task force he himself had set up and

vigorously appealed for education budget cuts. He sought to under-cut categorical aid programmes by consolidating them without appropriate legislation. One consequence of the rejection of the Pifer Report, together with the attempt to erode federal education monies and programmes, was the creation of the Emergency Committee for Full Funding. It was formed in 1969 to lobby for the blocking of President Nixon's priority of reducing categorical aid to education and all education funding. This lobby was composed of all the major education associations all of which agreed not to break ranks for partisan interests. It was therefore a considerable force.

A Nation at Risk, the report of the National Commission on Excellence in Education, gave the nation an insight into the condition and status of schooling and teaching in the United States. Its promulgation in 1983 created a political storm, and had the intended political effect of diverting attention from federal cutbacks in education by focusing on the 'mediocrity' in schooling.

Actually, Commission members were appointed by Secretary Bell, not by the White House. Thus, the Commission's Report, which created an unprecedented national debate, was not strictly speaking a presidential commisson. *A Nation at Risk* had a distribution of over three million copies, and for nearly a year was the Government's most sought-after document. Reagan was quick to take advantage of its audience, and his adoption of the Commission's report was a political coup. It exemplified Reagan's strategy of emphasising the problems of education, while simultaneously absolving the federal government from active participation and funding of those identified problems.

The Presidential Advisory Commission is another, more conspicuous method of eliciting suggestions and public support for possible policy adoption. It can be a potent political weapon, both in the power that resides in the president's right to appoint its members and in the strength of its advice to the president or public. President Nixon used the advisory commission to great advantage and astuteness by naming eight times as many members as his political mentor, Dwight Eisenhower, twice as many as Kennedy and nearly twice as many as Johnson.

President Nixon created such an education advisory commission in 1970. In his message to Congress he said:

I am today signing an Executive Order establishing a President's Commission on School Finance, to be in existence for two years, reporting to the President periodically on future revenue needs and fiscal priorities for public and non-public schools.

141

Nixon's presidential advisory commission attempted to discover 'the probable rate of growth in per-pupil expenditures in the coming decade and its consequences for tax policy, for educational finance and for educational quality'. It also set out to learn 'the implications of Federal revenue sharing for the financing of public and non-public education'.

The emphasis was on reform: 'This nation cannot continue to finance and distribute education as it has in the past. For many reasons — fiscal, legal, political, and moral — the system will have to change.' The reform premiss under which staff and commission members operated was radical — a sign of the times — but not necessarily antithetical to the education establishment which sensed the need for adaptations in all phases of schooling.

The concluding remarks of the skilful final report, *Schools, People and Money*, subtitled 'The Need for Education Reform', were daring and ambitious, as were the assumptions upon which the White House Report was grounded: the Commission began this report by asserting that 'for millions of children, American education — both public and nonpublic — is not working as it was intended to work.'

The chief policy advocated by the Commission was not lost on the Washington education establishment; the states were to be the principal actors in the educational reform movement. The Report recommended that the states re-assert their traditional pre-eminence in education and equalise funding within their jurisdictions. It followed that this would necessarily result in a weakening of emphasis on the receipt of federal funds by local schools and hence a reduction in the need for those categorical aid programmes in existence. John Fisher recognised this shift in policy and noted the divergence in a dissenting comment: 'The Commission's recommendations on the Federal role scarcely touch the one task on school finance that can be performed only by federal action — equalizing educational opportunity at a reasonable level *among* the States.' He alone noted, although several concurred, that what the Commission was recommending was actually a national reduction of programmes then designed to equalise opportunity. Fisher continued:

> Differences in wealth among the States are so wide that the poorer ones cannot support their schools adequately except by neglecting other public functions or by imposing much heavier taxes than the wealthier States require to provide good schools for their children.

The focus on distributing federal money equitably among the states which would then distribute it to localities was indeed a part of the overall Administration plan at general and special revenue-sharing. Chester Finn, a special assistant in the White House during the Nixon Administration, notes: 'Under a Nixon presidency, Washington would back away from the categorical programs that characterized federal education policy and also from the civil rights enforcement that accompanied such programs.' (Finn, 1977) Conceived as a broad policy statement on the truly critical need for educational reform, particularly in school finance, the President's Commission on School Finance was in fact a device for enunciating the broader presidential priority of revenue-sharing. The Commission's membership reflected that certitude. One bishop and the presidents of two Catholic universities were a testament to Nixon's desire to honour a commitment he had with Catholic educators on the parochial school question. A former governor was included. The one federal education representative was an avowed spokesman for states' rights in education. The chairman of the Commission was Chairman of the Board of a major multinational. Commission membership assured reasonable conformity with presidential priorities in general and education in particular.

PRESIDENTIAL APPOINTMENTS

A second strategy for policy development is that of presidential appointment. President Kennedy specifically chose to be Commissioner of Education, Francis Keppel, a man without the traditional education credentials, because he wanted a vigorous reform of the nation's federal education policy. Harold Howe, Keppel's successor as Commissioner, also had President Johnson's ear because Johnson sought education legislation as a chief Administration enterprise. Howe consequently received presidential encouragement — a valuable factor in Washington politics — for his suggestions; except on the occasion when he tried to enforce on Mayor Daley's Chicago new desegregation plans, in accordance with the new Civil Rights Act of 1964.

President Nixon's appointment of James Allen, who had declined the post earlier under Johnson, was welcomed with relief by educators. Allen was well regarded as Commissioner of Education in New York State and had been the Democratic Party's first choice as US Commissioner. His first interview with President Nixon after his appointment as he himself told the story to colleagues, was a presage of his political difficulties ahead. When Allen asked the President what he thought was the nation's foremost problem in education, Nixon responded after a pause and looked at the ceiling of the White House office, 'Mr Commissioner, what can we do about this discipline in the schools?' Allen then wished he had never taken the job.

As the crisis over school busing erupted, and inflation and the Vietnam war became political priorities, Allen was systematically ignored, his recommendations for chief US Office of Education officials delayed, and he was bereft of any education policy objectives from the White House. Allen decided to act. He announced in Los Angeles during a speech the creation of a Right to Read programme. It was a bold stroke of political fortune and it worked in his favour. It was the kind of move Nixon himself might have made. The President telephoned and offered his congratulations and endorsed the programme. There was, of course, no congressional authorisation for the programme and no budgetary allocation. However, largely because of the forceful persuasiveness of Ruth Love its first director, the Right to Read programme was later to be accorded high visibility in the Nixon Administration, although it never received more than $10 million annually.

Allen's action demonstrates that the President can appoint but he cannot always control. The final straw with Commissioner Allen came during a press conference. He was asked by a reporter what he, as an educator, thought of the Vietnam war. Allen replied that he had a private opinion but that his public office was not the proper forum for making it known. The reporter persisted and Allen committed the sin that is the nightmare of every public official: he publicly voiced his dissent with Administration policy. It was his private opinion, he had cautioned, but he aired it to the press and he was swiftly asked for his resignation.

A president can influence education policy by making appointments in other places than the US Department of Education. The Executive Office of the President usually has a special assistant in charge of education. Presidents Kennedy and Nixon assigned an aide to education only if the occasion demanded it. But President Johnson's interest in education, as befits a former teacher, was continuous and not just peripheral, and Joseph Califano, later to become Secretary of HEW under President Carter, was Johnson's special education advisor.

Daniel Moynihan, former Professor of Education and Urban Affairs at Harvard, Ambassador to India, later Senator from New York, was President Nixon's Executive Secretary of the Council on Urban Affairs and Special Assistant on Domestic Policy. He clearly had a large hand in drafting the two major education messages President

Nixon sent to Congress in March, 1970. He noted in the Foreword to *Education and the Presidency*: 'The two presidential messages that emerged from this process were . . . the most comprehensive and credible statements of their kind ever to have been sent to the Congress.' (Finn, 1977)

His description of the relative importance of education in the national order of presidential priorities is apt because Moynihan himself was responsible for initiating and seeking the President's support for his education intentions. This could only happen because of his position as a presidential appointee and, one must add, his stature in the academic community. He continues:

> Education? At the top of the agenda of issues that most concern the American public? Well, yes. In these months — two or three years really — education issues for once had seized the public mind and the subject became political as it had scarcely been before and has not been since.

Earlier presidential pronouncements had assumed that schools should produce children of achievement and learning skills; the Nixon Administration was to make this the cornerstone of its educational policy. That particular view became the dominant one because of one person in the White House: Counselor to the President, Daniel P. Moynihan.

One idea had dominated Moynihan's thinking with regard to schools and schooling. It was that the conclusions of the Coleman Report, the study commissioned by the Civil Rights Act of 1964 'concerning the lack of availability of equal educational oppportunities for individuals by reason of race, color, religion or national origin in public educational institutions', should form the basis for future educational financing. The Coleman Report was the second largest social science research project ever undertaken. The findings demonstrated that of all school variables teachers are the most important, but that students differ in achievement and ability more because of home background and outside influences than they do because of school influences.

Finn comments on how Moynihan's thinking influenced education policy under Nixon:

> There must, after all, be some reason why another federal program is worth having and that reason must have something to do with what children learn — it was Moynihan's view that three years

after the Coleman Report the time had come for the president to be explicit: the nation should regard its schools, with or without federal dollars in them, in terms of their productivity.

Nearly every president has made disappointing appointments to executive positions, some of which have been politically embarrassing. The Reagan Administration may have been determined not to be embarrassed in this way. However, it did bring political loyalty to a new level as a test of executive competence. Never before in the history of American politics was ideology so overtly the criterion for administrative acceptance. In some cases, the Reagan Administration appointed to positions of executive and public trust people whose avowed aim was the abolition of the agency they administered. This was true of Ted Bell, former Secretary of Education. While in the Carter Administration, Bell had vigorously advocated the creation of a cabinet-level department; in the Reagan Administration he sought to dismantle the very programmes he had previously defended. In the end, Bell talked Reagan out of abolishing the Department and spoke out in favour of education issues.

USE OF AGENCIES

A third strategy is the president's use of federal agencies. The Office of Management and Budget is the most convenient for this purpose because it is the means of controlling the budget for education programmes. A president can also employ the immediate office of the Secretary or Assistant Secretary, either of which can become the nucleus of policy formulation for legislation or executive action.

The president can create new agencies, as President Johnson did with the Office of Economic Opportunity (OEO) and President Nixon for the National Institute of Education. He can transfer programmes, as Nixon did with OEO.

The president can also bypass the bureaucracy entirely, to control policy directives, by establishing a 'working group', a somewhat formalised task force but one composed only of inside trusted lieutenants. Until the report is released, policy is a mystery — and thus immune from formative criticism. The members may actually be key officials *within* the bureaucracy or they may be presidential appointees. Yet they operate outside the normal channels of supervision and communication. The president in fact controls the 'working group'.

146

The 'working group', by the nature of its composition and secrecy, may become the focus for conflict, not because of the substance of its deliberations, but because of its inaccessibility.

When administration officials iron out problems before sending the bill off, they, not the Congress, become the focus for conflict resolution. Administration officials are then in a stronger position to control and shape the policy agenda based on their proposals, and they enhance the opportunity to give up the least of their ideals and save the most. This procedure steals away congressional prerogative and power in policy making. (Summerfield, 1974)

Sometimes the manner of deliberation is not always as orderly or as rational as the discussants would like. When men are face to face with the President of the United States their minds are swayed by the presence of a man who can alter global destinies:

We explained our recommendations to the President. At the beginning, the meeting seemed to proceed in an orderly and satisfactory way. However, as people talked, as the President raised probing questions, minds and opinions began to change again, and not only on small points . . . For some, it was from one extreme to another. (Kennedy, 1971)

This account is from *Thirteen Days, A Memoir of the Cuban Missile Crisis*, one of the most tense and electrifying periods of American history and government. The possibility of war was imminent, and government leaders were faced with choosing strategies which could conceivably lead to their own destruction. The Executive Committee, as it was known, was formed by President Kennedy and reported directly to him. For those two weeks it *was* the government. Robert Kennedy narrates its working format:

During all these deliberations, we all spoke as equals. There was no rank, and, in fact, we did not even have a chairman . . . As a result . . . the conversations were completely uninhibited and unrestricted . . . It was a tremendously advantageous procedure that does not frequently occur within the executive branch of government, where rank is often so important.

What is the best way for a president to receive the most valuable advice on matters he deems significant? Education will not compare with nuclear war in a hierarchy of administrative decisions. However, if the procedures of government in crisis can help streamline the way in which the president receives advice and counsel, the format can be duplicated in other working sessions. Robert Kennedy comments again on his perceptions as a participant and observer of that drama:

> I believe our deliberations proved conclusively how important it is that the President have the recommendations and opinions of more than one individual, of more than one department, of more than one point of view. Opinion, even fact itself, can best be judged by conflict, by debate.

A president can also 'use' an agency by ignoring its services. By failing to involve an agency or any of its key personnel in policy decisions likely to affect it, the president or his representatives can eviscerate a federal agency. This occurred when the decision was made to transfer educational research and development out of the Office of Education in the early 1970s and to begin a new education agency, later to become the National Institute of Education. No research personnel in the Office of Education participated in strategies for forming the new agency, and Office of Education personnel were specifically excluded from becoming employed in the new National Institute of Education. The nucleus of the new agency's personnel came from other government agencies: the acting temporary head had come from Systems Development Corporation; the second acting director came from the Office of Management and Budget; the first permanent director, an economist not an educational researcher by training, came from the Office of Economic Opportunity.

On the other hand, President Franklin Roosevelt in 1935 used, to the alarm of many, a newly created federal agency to further education. The Works Project Administration supported scores of education programmes that bypassed state governments. It was the first instance in which federal funds were used for educational purposes and not included in grants to the states.

MESSAGES TO CONGRESS

The message to Congress, usually on the 'State of the Union', has been the customary manner of satisfying the constitutional requirement. The State of the Union address serves as a political and policy outline of later, more well-developed legislative recommendations.

However, education is rarely mentioned in a president's State of the Union address and so the special education message is the primary vehicle for enunciating education policy.

Education messages are developed by White House staff in conjunction with selected Administration officials. President Nixon sent two education messages, one on elementary and secondary education and one on higher education. Both were written with consummate skill and were comprehensive in scope. President Carter's first education message in February 1978 recommended a Department of Education, which he had promised in the campaign and had mentioned in the State of the Union address.

A comparison of Nixon's first education message to Congress in March 1970 and Carter's in February 1978 will illustrate areas of similarity and points of departure in the formulation of federal education policy. The Nixon document is more sweeping and detailed than Carter's. Revenue-sharing dominates the total Nixon strategy. It was his chief ingredient for federal funding patterns, and so we find a preoccupation with school funding and the creation of a Commission on School Finance. There is no Carter Strategy for the federal role in education.

The messages are also similar in predictable ways. The two principal forms of student aid — compensatory education for elementary students and grants and loans for college students — attest to these perennial problems. The issue of some assistance to non-public or private school students also appears in both messages and will always be a federal education concern. Carter's message dealt with necessary legislative changes but there was no overall theme, such as the New Federalism of the Nixon era, by which to gauge future policy development.

Presidential messages, as a primary expression of Administration policy in education, have over the past 120 years been aimed principally at illiteracy among elementary school children. Johnson's insistence on it and Nixon's and Carter's inclusion of it are testimony to that executive effort. It is therefore safe to presume that aid to students poor in basic skills, whose parents are thus likely to be poor in income, will always receive priority in presidential messages. Similarly, college student grants and loans have taken precedence over institutional grants-in-aid, and there is no evidence that the trend is likely to be reversed.

APPEAL TO THE PUBLIC: THE WHITE HOUSE CONFERENCES

Because it gets a press briefing, the education message is also an appeal to the voting public for support of Administration policies. But every ten years an unusual opportunity comes for a president to draw upon public and professional education advice: the White House Conference on Children and Youth.

The tradition began with President Theodore Roosevelt. It has now eclipsed all other conferences sponsored by the White House in both size and number of participants and sessions. When held, it dominates the education focus of the administration sponsoring it, even though usually no major legislation appears. It has become a national forum for education discussion about children and youth and many of its discussants mistakenly believe they are formulating federal education policy by participating.

At the turn of the century Homer Folks (1900) wrote a monograph entitled, *The Care of Destitute, Neglected and Delinquent Children*. It caused a stir and was to have a profound effect on later developments in education, for the controversy it generated resulted in the White House Conference on Dependent Children in 1909. 'Home life is the highest and finest product of civilization', began the report. President Taft signed the Act creating the Children's Bureau in the Department of Labor which the conference had recommended. The conference urged that funds for its recommendations be made available from private and public reserves.

The second White House Conference was called by President Wilson in 1919. Eight regional conferences followed. The main feature was not so much the conference's recommendations, but that the conference was held at all in the immediate aftermath of the war. From then on there was to be a decennial conference on children.

President Hoover himself opened the White House Conference on Child Health and Protection in 1930, the most productive of all the conferences. He said: 'The fundamental purpose of this Conference is to set forth an understanding of those safeguards which will assure to them, the children, health in mind and body.' The conference addressed the questions of medical services, public health and administration, education and training, and the handicapped. It stressed again the importance of the family in educating the child.

The first White House Conference in 1909 is generally credited with accelerating the progress of state legislation for mothers' pensions and child welfare organisations. But during Hoover's Administration, the White House Conference had money ($500,000 in 1930 was a great deal), research planners and enthusiastic delegates. It achieved not only the participation of a large number of professionals (1,200), but also the establishment of the *modus operandi* for future White House Conferences.

President Franklin Roosevelt's White House Conference on Children in a Democracy in 1940 focused on medical attention to the child and its family. It urged preventive care throughout the country, especially for the poor. Its call was for an expansion of public health facilities, financed through the general tax funds. It also recommended the appointment of a committee to develop a policy for national standards of nutrition.

President Roosevelt commented that the conference should also address the urgent task of strengthening democracy:

> Adequate national defense calls for educated citizens. Yes, I agree with you that public assistance of many kinds is necessary. But I suggest to you that the Federal treasury has a bottom to it, and that mere grants-in-aid constitute no permanent solution of the problem of our health, our education, or our children.

Although his Administration was the New Deal, he did not want the federal government responsible for solving all societal ills.

President Harry Truman opened the White House Conference on Child Welfare in 1950 with these remarks:

> It is good to see that we can pursue a goal of such moment through a conference such as this. In this unique demonstration of our democracy's concern for its children, there is proof again that our American tradition of free exchange of fact and opinion is a living, working force.

When President Johnson called the 1965 White House Conference on Children and Youth there were 6,700 participants, 210 workshops and 670 recommendations. The behemoth conference had taken over the format at the expense of substance. Attendance was now more important for participants than the outcomes, and occasionally the proceedings verged on the ridiculous. William Carr, once executive secretary of the National Education Association, tested his growing scepticism of the conference by proposing a set of resolutions for the 1965 conference. They were hooted down and pooh-poohed. Then he explained that they had been recommended and passed by the 1930 White House Conference.

The children of one age become the adults of the next generation. There was trepidation on the eve of the 1970 White House Conference that the nation's youth would use the formal occasion to demonstrate against President Nixon's war policies. So two conferences were planned: one for children and one for youth.

The White House Conference on Youth in 1971, which did in fact become a forum for dissent and expressions of cynicism, was held in Estes Park, Colorado, a mountain setting far removed from the communications and media of a large metropolis. The White House Conference on Children was a stage for educational actors and yielded nothing that was not known in research or practice. Some wanted to rescue something from it, and Senator Mondale helped create a sub-committee to see if conference recommendations could be synthesised into a manageable federal programme. This Senate exercise came to naught.

The White House Conference began as a forum for educational experts deliberating on a relevant and timely concern. It then developed into an unwieldy assembly with unrealistic expectations. It finally resulted in confrontations between the Administration and its critics. The singular importance of the conference was lost through unmanageable repetition.

10

Administering Federal Education

It is expressly contended to belong to the discretion of the National Legislature to pronounce upon the objects which concern the *general welfare*, and for which under that description an appropriate sum of money is requisite and proper. And there seems to be no room for a doubt that whatever concerns the general interests of *learning of agriculture* of manufacturers, and of commerce, are within the spheres of national councils, *as far as regards an application of money.*

James Madison, *Report on the Virginia Resolutions of 1798* (emphasis Madison's)

The pull of competing interests and objectives — executive edicts, judicial opinions and decrees and Congressional power and influence — make up the diversity of educational policy formation in action and are illustrative of democracy at work. No branch of government controls all the variables. School desegregation was born in the Supreme Court. The Elementary and Secondary Education Act was born in the White House and the Congress over court-ordered busing demonstrations.

There is another part of government, not altogether illusive or invisible, though some would call it impenetrable, that makes the wheels of legislation go around. This chapter is about the people who administer federal education laws. It is about the executives, officers, civil servants, bureaucrats, who technically work for the chief executive but who none the less manage the nation's federal education budget. It concerns their status, their role, power and influence in the management of legislated policy.

There is on the one hand, the development of policy which results in legislation, but there is also the administration of policy once legislation is enacted. If there were no laws there would be no bureaucracy. It is the management of policy, of educational legislative administration, that is the subject of this chapter.

Two distinctions are important in what follows about the bureaucracy: the first about policy, and the second about people.

We have already seen the difference between judicial and legislative policy, and we must now further identify *administrative* policy, which may come either directly from the chief executive or from the agency designated to administer the law. All federal administrative agencies have their organisational structures determined by law or statute. However, they are also given some autonomy for establishing procedures and courses of action for defining their legislated authority. Sometimes the agency head is given broad discretionary powers to implement the law. For example, when civil rights' proponents finally broke a Senate filibuster and the Civil Rights Act was passed in 1964, the law gave the then Office of Education broad authority to assist schools in desegregating. It also authorised the Attorney General to intervene in private suits brought by people allegedly discriminated against if the case was judged to be of 'general public importance'.

Consequently, the process of implementing policy can become an established *modus operandi* — a policy in itself. Sometimes this administrative policy comes under public criticism and review, as did the poverty issues in the Office of Economic Opportunity, the Central Intelligence Agency's (CIA) operational procedures, or HEW's withdrawal of federal funds for a school's failure to desegregate.

The second distinction is between the *career personnel* who administer federal education laws and the *political executives* — only about 200 in federal government — whom the president appoints with the advice and consent of the Senate. Although political appointees are technically supervisors and high-level managers, their real authority is somewhat circumscribed by the career bureaucrats and technicians who actually manage the myriad programmes. Such people have common interests, perhaps even common personality traits. The memoirs of public servants make fascinating reading. One such autobiography, that of John Beames, a British Civil Servant in India in the nineteenth century, reveals something of the way all government employees view their jobs and presents a commonly shared experience of federal or public service. Of interest is his perception of the administration of the laws:

> It cannot be repeated too often that the difficulty lies not in the laws and rules that are promulgated, but in getting them carried out. It is not always easy, I admit, to make a law which exactly meets the requirements of all the complicated systems . . . and other matters which occur . . . This law so elaborately worded, these provisions the result of so much anxious deliberation, must now be enforced all over the country. (Beames, 1961)

This could be a contemporary statement about the state of affairs governing federal education programme administration from a school's point of view. Little has changed in government management.

Education policy can originate in any branch of the federal government. The development of federal education policy is an interactive process between the executive, legislative and judicial branches. It is initiated by one of the three and not unusually opposed by either or both of the remaining branches. The Supreme Court orders busing, the Congress attempts to pass laws stopping it. The president tries to impound federal dollars, the Congress passes stiffer laws prohibiting him. The president tries to package legislation in education (calling it revenue sharing) and the Congress makes him back off.

Sometimes presidents are novices, as President Carter was, unaware of how policy implementation flows through the monstrously complex bureaucracy, from the political appointees to the obscure managers who make or break the programme. An education programme manager has the desire to increase personal and professional status in the management of education policy. A bureaucrat's first obligation is the protection of status, a well-defined pecking order within the organisation, through department, bureau, division, branch, section. Once secure in career tenure, and after years of seasoning and confidence in the network of personnel contacts, only then can a bureaucrat demonstrate his prestige. Prestige increases with the ability to manipulate the power of the organisation itself.

When educators enter the world of government bureaucracy they are infants in organisational influence. They must learn the art of combining their interests and talents with those of the agency. Their competence is not in question; only their loyalty to the organisation. In fact, the bureaucracy could not function at all if many bureaucrats pursued independent ambitions, like political appointees, under the protection of the organisation.

Political appointees may have been effective managers in private industry, but they do not remain long enough to learn federal government procedures, understand other career officials or probe the innumerable avenues of effective management of federal policies, laws and programmes. 'Political executives are not likely to be in any position for very long. Career executives, on the other hand, have an average tenure of fifteen years in public civil service.' (Heclo, 1977) In education, for example, in the ten-year period 1968-78 there were five Commissioners of Education: Howe, Allen, Marland, Bell and Boyer.

It is the middle-management bureaucrat, who argues for policy continuity with any change in administration or with new political appointees, who know the laws, the programmes, the personnel system. The most important item managed is federal money.

THE ECONOMICS OF THE BUREAUCRACY:
GRANTS AND CONTRACTS

The executive view of the management of federal education consists of planning, soliciting, evaluating and awarding government grants and contracts. Most awards are *contracts*, binding agreements between two parties, one of which is always the government. The contract goes to a school, college or university, state agency or non-profit organisation to carry out a stipulated agreement. A *grant*, on the other hand, is a conditional gift from the government to an organisation or individual to conduct research or do a study.

The only authorised government official designated to formalise a contractual agreement on behalf of the government is the *grants* or *fiscal officer*. The *programme officer* is responsible for the technical monitoring of the agreement between the government and the recipient.

There is an established history of precedents for the awarding of contracts and grants, arcane to many and a terror to most. Congressional legislation consists not only of bills and acts, but of clauses which contain provisions for 'regulations', which agencies issue under this authority. Statements like the following are commonplace: 'The grant which a local educational agency . . . is eligible to receive shall be determined pursuant to such criteria as the Commissioner determines will best carry out the purposes of this title.' The Acts of Congress are published in the *United States Statutes at Large*. All regulations, executive orders and proclamations are published in the *Federal Register*, published daily during the working week. Those regulations which are still in force are published in the *Code of Federal Regulations*.

These regulations spell out the manner of submitting a proposal for contract consideration and the method for evaluation. Consultant evaluators judge each proposal according to these regulatory items. Depending on the money available to each programme, projects likely to receive funding are ranked and checked for geographic disbursement. The spread of projects somewhat evenly throughout the country is both a political expedient and often a legislative requirement. The Metric Education Program, for example, considered small for a national education effort, in the fiscal year 1978 had an appropriation of $2,090,000. For that amount it received 475 proposals totalling over $10 million in requests. It funded only 64.

Prospective award winners are notified — their congressmen are told the day before by telegram — and a period of negotiation begins.

The grants officer must ensure that the terms and conditions for receiving government funds are met and the programme officer checks for the conformity of the proposal with the law and regulations. Negotiable items include: the rental of equipment, the possible transfer of funds from one line-item in the budget to another, travel expenses, subcontracting with consultants, personnel changes, the publication of materials — often including copyright procedures and similar budget topics. In the meantime, however, letters of credit allowing the recipient to draw on government funds are awarded. In the concluding phase of negotiation, the final budget figure and length of time to complete the project are determined. Negotiation always results in a fixed-price contract when the award is made and the specifications agreed upon. The programme officer periodically monitors, by phone and on-site visitation, the project performance.

When a proposal is submitted it is proprietary information. Once funded, the contract falls in the public domain. Although the contract document is public, the budget and negotiated information remains confidential. When Congress appropriates funds for an educational programme, the administration of the programme reverts to the executive branch. Occasionally, a *continuing resolution*, a congressional act which authorises spending at the level of the preceding year, is enacted to conduct federal business while the Congress, and the Congress and the Administration, debate the merits of new funding-levels.

The Executive Office of Management and Budget then appoints the money, after it too has held hearings and justifications from the government agencies. Each agency then allots the segmented money to the differing levels of bureaucracy. It is usually parcelled out according to salary and expense money, administrative costs and contract and grant awards. Unexpended funds revert each year to the Treasury.

Perhaps the most controversial education programme, and therefore the most difficult to administer, was the student assistance programme. Actually, there were two such programmes. One was the Basic Educational Opportunity Grants, called the Pell Grants after the Democratic Senator who initiated it, and the other was the Guaranteed Student Loan programme. The former provided awards to undergraduate students who demonstrated need. The latter provided subsidised loans for any post-secondary student regardless of need.

Over a period of time the original purpose of the Pell Grants was extended from 'demonstrated need' to include almost anyone who wanted a student loan. For example, changes had been made that permitted students whose parents earned in excess of $30,000 to draw upon the programme's resources. There were, as always in such large programmes with discretionary authorities, minor and major scandals. Some student-loan money was spent for non-educational purposes and there was a high default-rate. In fact, according to one Department of Justice official, the federal government lost more money in student-loan defaults than it had in bank robberies during the entire century.

Until the Reagan Administration, the federal government's role in education had usually taken the form of categorical programmes. There was a proliferation of education laws with individual appropriations, which had generated separate regulations and requirements, created whole new interest groups and clientele, and promoted the growth of distinct administrative structures for each programme at federal, state and local levels.

The rationale for the new political and administrative strategy was not difficult to comprehend. All agreed that federal education programmes had become complex, duplicative and even counterproductive. An adversarial relationship had begun to develop among differing educational authorities. The marriage was breaking up.

THE POLITICS OF THE BUREAUCRACY: CIVIL SERVANTS AND BUREAUCRATS

The Civil Service Commission was created in 1883 by Congress to establish a personnel system for appointments to federal positions based on competition and merit, not political or personal preference. It is the primary federal agency concerned with the people who work in government, their recruitment and examination, personnel practices, employee development and training, awards and benefits and retirement.

Although certain agencies, like the Atomic Energy Commission, National Aeronautics and Space Administration and the Post Office, are exempt from civil service regulations, all federal education personnel are governed by its practices. A study of the people who manage such programmes would be incomplete without a knowledge of the institutional forces regulating its activities.

The civil service is not a normal bureaucracy. Its existence is grounded on unambiguous principles. The idea is to protect career officials from political control, while instilling in them a sense of loyalty to the federal agency employing them. They give their allegiance to a politically appointed agency head. In return they receive, provided there is evidence of continuingly satisfactory performance, secure tenure. The price they pay is the need to respond to the sudden changes in policy as executive Administrations come and go, and the continued commitment they must bring to the new policy and politically motivated agency leadership. Big, unwieldy and cumbersome as government is, this shared loyalty to the functioning of government and the administration of the nation's laws, together with a belief in the integrity and competency of the staff, maintain the agency and strengthen the feeling of accomplishment.

There are also informal established networks, relationships between present and former federal officials who can assist with administrative and policy circumstances: an executive officer who can expedite a travel voucher; a sympathetic programme officer knowledgeable in contracting techniques; a friend in a national education organisation who can raise an issue with a higher official. These relationships, needless to say, are cultivated only through long experience in the Washington education establishment.

Interpersonal forces are perhaps the strongest in the determination of federal education policy. Key career officials, senior legislative aides, influential association secretaries, a few congressmen, all know each other and can silently activate or kill changes in policy. There is a common bond, a sharing of government power in the public trust that welds together the varying competencies and characteristics of these politicians and career officials. The same kind of *esprit de corps* forges any professional working group.

In the disillusionment following the Nixon resignation, what was tarnished most was the image of the integrity of government to function on behalf of the common weal. The concept of public servant was likewise blotched. It was as if it had suddenly been discovered that the teacher had all along been stealing the children's lunch money.

One example from 1972 will illustrate the working of the bureaucracy in the US Office of Education, as it was then known. The Nixon Administration attempted a strategy for gaining control of educational programmes by combining several pieces of congressional legislation. This was called Educational Renewal.

The Nixon Administration packaged categorical aid programmes intended for elementary and secondary schools. The Administration planned to control selected pieces of separate education legislation by placing them under the administrative umbrella of revenue-sharing. This emphasis on reform disguised the subtle executive manoeuvre to control congressional policy in education.

As a management device there was good sense in a strategy designed to combine separate programmes intended generally for children of low-income families. As Congress viewed it, however, it was a plan to gain executive control of district programmes which Congress had legislated and funded. It was a struggle of the executive versus the legislative over national education programmes. In the end Congress won, and several bureaucrats paid for that victory with their jobs.

The federal education officer must make decisions that go beyond trained competence, having to manage the project's operations to ensure that it adheres to the specifications proposed in the grant document. The politics of this enterprise is the delicate art of reconciling competing differences for limited funds. The bureaucracy is the indispensible means of translating education policy into results.

J.J. Servan-Schreiber (1979) points to the dilemma: 'Americans are not more intelligent than other people. Yet human factors — the ability to adapt easily, flexibility of organizations, the creative power of teamwork — are the key to their success.' What happens when the individual encounters government bureaucracy known for its uniformity, rigidity and inflexibility? For the professional educator in the education bureaucracy of the federal government, the result may be professional and personal conflict. David Stanley (1964) says of these officials:

> The scope and impact of their responsibilities demand that they be *superior professionals and executives* — not merely adequate ones . . . and as scientists, professionals and executives they must demonstrate skill and knowledge that will command the respect of the top men in their fields; they must therefore have flexibility, a high innovative capacity, a sharp critical faculty, and ability to synthesize and integrate.

What we have most to fear about a federal education bureaucracy is what we have to fear about any power source — too much faith in its policies or pomp. The more power, the more caution we need. The mystique of governmental superiority, however, has had its periodic deflation — the Bay of Pigs, Vietnam, Watergate, the near-impeachment of an incumbent president, the failure of the Iranian rescue mission. Are bureaucrats any less prone to error even with all their access to information and the apparatus of government? Somewhere between the myth of bureaucratic omnipotence and the wounded vanity of bureaucratic bungling lies the reality of the work-a-day world of the federal education worker.

On the other hand, and in fairness, federal education managers can only administer the legislated policy, and that policy is often poorly co-ordinated. All the necessary personnel needed to administer legislated programmes are not available, nor are all the support systems present or operative. Much of a federal bureaucrat's time is spent drawing up regulations, reviewing regulations, reviewing proposals, negotiating contracts, evaluating progress and repeating the whole process each year. There never is enough money to evaluate projects funded on-site.

The nation's federal workers are periodically vilified, pilloried, and ridiculed. In a democracy the public is entitled to know the mistakes of public workers. Their occasional bumbling, their unreadable regulations make good press copy. Public servants in general are the standard butt of satirists and cartoonists.

11

Managing Federal Schools

That it be recommended to the respective Assemblies and Conventions of the United Colonies, where no government sufficient to the exigencies of their affairs have been hitherto established, to adopt such a government as shall, in the opinion of the representatives of the people, best conduce to the happiness and safety of their constituents in particular, and America in general.

Journals of Congress, May 1776

The most familiar and conspicuous education programmes of the federal government are those sponsored by congressional legislation and administered by executive agencies such as the US Dept of Education and the National Science Foundation. It comes as a surprise to many educators to learn of the extensiveness of federal schools and federally sponsored schools. Even among researchers of the federal education involvement — like Ginsburg and Turnbull (1981), who mistakenly say 'The federal government does not run schools' — the federal operation of schools has been traditionally overlooked.

EDUCATION AND NATIONAL SECURITY: MILITARY SCHOOLS

The single most significant influence in the history of the relationship between education and the federal government has been national security.

Much legislation in the name of defence or national security has directly aided servicemen, veterans or refugees. The first education provision for refugees was passed in 1865. The Act provided for a Bureau of Refugees in the War Department, a federal service organisation to help support freed slaves with food, clothing and education for citizenship.

A second defence-related education act originated with the return of veterans in 1918. The Smith-Sears Act of 1918 provided for training programmes for returning World War I veterans. It also gave stipends, dependent allowances and support, and provided for counselling and vocational rehabilitation and placement. In the ten years of its existence, approximately 180,000 veterans benefited. The

Federal Board of Vocational Education which administered the programme did not contract out for services to educational institutions, as would be done today. Instead, it hired instructors, designed courses and even created facilities. No one objected to this kind of federal control in 1918, and the programme did not clash with established college and university vocational training programmes.

In 1930 Congress established the Veterans Administration (VA). The VA had the authority to establish schools on its own, as did the Federal Board for Vocational Education, but chose not to. The Serviceman's Readjustment Act of 1944 and the GI Bill of Rights propelled millions of veterans from World War II back into classrooms and brought aobut an explosive renascence in college life.

During the late 1940s nearly 90 per cent of all students receiving federal education funds were veterans. More than half of all veterans in World War II (15.3 million) received some kind of educational assistance. The total appropriation was over $15.5 billion.

This national security and defence-related objective was, of course, a political ploy, but it satisfied the contemporary demand for educational rehabilitation. Congress responded with an act that facilitated the transition to peacetime employment.

In a similar way, the Civilian Conservation Corps (CCC), approved in 1937, had provided federal employment opportunities, mainly to youths, but also to veterans and American Indians, for the conservation of natural resources. The conservation camps were administratively under the control of the army, again underscoring the military involvement in federally sponsored education programmes. During World War II the Corps, instead of working on reclamation projects, shifted instead to defence projects on military reservations and the protection of forests. Many achieved literacy and numeracy through CCC, and others completed a secondary school education who would not otherwise have been able to.

For the young who were not participants in CCC, however, other federal opportunities existed. One was the National Youth Administration, a part of the Works Progress Administration. This youth branch — Lyndon Johnson was President Roosevelt's Texas administrator — provided work training for unemployed youth and students aged 16 to 25 who had dropped out of school. The programme helped thousands by opening up part-time work opportunities and allowing them the chance to earn enough money to continue their education. The federal government in fact operated schools, paid the students for working in them and administered their education.

If we charted the course of national emergencies — war, economic depression, crises in government — we would also be observing a parallel explosion of federal educational assistance programmes. In times of national crisis, despite the traditional role of state and local agencies in education, the federal government consistently sponsored schools, developed curricula and designed programmes and new organisations to administer them. Each intervention has had its corresponding economic impact, especially on manpower but also on construction and curriculum improvements.

The national reaction to Soviet space and weapons technology has influenced the federal response to education, the most notable of which was the National Defense Education Act of 1958. This was the culmination of a series of federal education investments that had already been established by tradition: military schools and academies, vocational rehabilitation for veterans, the GI Bill, aid to orphans of veterans, the distribution of military surplus property to schools and training progammes for youth essential to national security.

'The Defense Department', according to former Defense Secretary Robert McNamara, 'is the largest single educational complex in history.' In 26 countries around the world, the Defense Department operates nearly 270 elementary, and junior and senior high schools. It employs over 9,000 teachers for a student population of approximately 150,000. Yet the schools operated for dependents of military personnel are actually only a small part of the Defense Department's total educational programme. During a five-year period in the mid-1960s, an annual average of 95,000 military personnel earned the high school equivalency diploma through the Defense Department.

Because only about 14 per cent of the more than three million in the armed forces actually qualify to fire weapons, the majority are relied upon for their technical skills. The Defense Department conducts professional and technical training in 1,500 different skill areas in more than 2,000 different courses. Correspondence courses enrol more than one million students.

Although this vast, global educational network operates primarily for the needs of the Defense Department, there are distinct societal advantages. Annually, nearly half a million trained servicemen and women return to civilian life bringing with them *skills that were not paid for by local or state governments*. As an example, many of the Federal Aviation Administration's air traffic controllers, who scan and monitor the nation's commercial corridors of the air, were originally trained in the military and worked at military airports. Ex-military personnel return to civilian life with skills useful in medicine, electronics, engineering, transportation management, airplane and motor maintenance, construction trades and similar occupations essential to national progress.

In many instances, the Defense Department pioneered innovative programmes, particularly in educational technology. Programmed instruction techniques and closed-circuit television were a part of regular military training by the late 1960s. As early as 1969 at the US Naval Academy in Annapolis, the entire engineering and science curriculum was packaged into programmed-learning units on computer-assisted instructional systems. An undergraduate midshipman could learn physics, mathematics and chemistry and some engineering at his own pace. Such courses are now standard, but many were originally pioneered at military installations.

In addition to education legislation in the name of national security, and the Department of Defense schools, the military also operates its own service academies and joint service schools like the National War College and the Armed Forces Staff College. These service schools, joint service schools and advanced management schools operate in addition to the three major service academies for undergraduates leading to a degree and a commission: the US Air Force Academy, the US Military Academy and the US Naval Academy.

Military education programmes under the auspices of the Department of Defense are the largest educator of skilled personnel in the world. Throughout American history, national security and defence policy have been enormously influential in determining the response, the form and the purposes of the federal role in education. Joel Spring has extensively analysed the way in which national education issues have been shaped by manpower and defence strategies. Schools for military dependents, defence service schools and joint agency schools are thus a major influence over the role of the federal government in education.

EDUCATION AND THE AMERICAN INDIAN

Although few Americans are aware of this, American Indians live in all 50 states, speak over 300 different languages, and are extraordinarily diverse ethnically. Contrary to common understanding, twice as many live off federal reservations as live on them.

This history of the federal policy towards American Indians, including and especially education policy, constitutes a national tragedy of the first magnitude. Federal schools for Indians constitute some of the oldest in the nation: there were 37 Indian schools as early as 1842 when the new Bureau of Indian Affairs was created in the War Department. The education policy was an extension of the policy towards Indians in general, namely forced assimilation and expropriation of Indian land. The Homestead Act of 1863 reputedly opened up more land to settlers, and the commonest means of forcing Indians to relinquish more of their land was extermination of the buffalo herds, their main source of meat. This starved them into reservations, sited always on the most undesirable land available. The Dawes Severalty Act of 1887, known as the Allotment Act, was an attempt to offer land to Indians under the same conditions as to whites in the hopes of completing the break-up of Indian treaty land. It was one of the more odious pieces of national legislation, like the Alien and Sedition Acts, and in fact reduced the Indian land claims from 140 million acres (37 million ha) to less than 50 million acres (20 million ha) in 46 years.

The education policy, like the land policy, was to undermine tribal culture, by uprooting the American Indians from the homeland and enforcing a disciplined education process in a boarding school environment. Both federal boarding schools under the control of the Bureau of Indian Affairs and schools run by missions — which at one time under Grant's administration actually had control of the appointment of agents on the reservation — were intended to strip the Indian child of his culture and substitute English language and American mores in its place. These school costs were borne by the money appropriated from the land allotments. The social and cultural disintegration of the family and the tribe quickly followed these misconceived and misdirected policies. Federal boarding schools for American Indian students have been universally maligned by the Indian communities and in all reports about them. The goal of 'Americanising' students may have been in part acceptable to the immigrant population, but clearly was not to the indigenous one.

In a few states the education of Indian children rests with the state and not the federal government; but most American Indian children attend public schools with other non-Indian children. Only a small percentage now attend mission and other private schools.

'The responsibility for the education of Indian children', according to the 1969 Special Subcommittee Report on Indian Education chaired by Senator Ted Kennedy, 'is primarily in the hands of the Federal Government.' Two-thirds of all American Indian children receive some kind of federal education assistance — one-third from federal funds for Bureau of Indian Affairs schools, and one-third under federal funds authorised under the Johnson-O'Malley Act of 1934 for Indian children to attend public schools. Moreover, American Indian students receive special funds under many other categorical programmes.

A special word is needed about the Johnson-O'Malley Act passed by Congress in 1934 and amended in 1936. The original purpose was to confer upon the Secretary of the Interior the authority to contract with state-supported scools, colleges and universities for Indian education services. It was to 'arrange for the handling of certain Indian problems in which the Indian tribal life is largely broken up and in which the Indians are to a considerable extent mixed with the general population'. Education was one of those areas. Therefore, the legislation noted that 'it becomes advisable to fit them into the general public school scheme rather than to provide separate schools for them'. Johnson-O'Malley is one of the principal vehicles for subsidising education by the federal government for Indian children. The Act has been narrowly interpreted: funding criteria do not apply to Indians who have left the reservation.

American Indian children, for federal aid purposes, are defined as one-quarter or more Indian blood, and all Alaskan natives. In the fiscal year 1976 — the last year in which reasonably accurate data were available — there were 216,168 Indian students aged five to 18 enrolled in public, federal, private and mission schools. Comparatively, this would make the total student population, were it grouped in one locale, the eighth-largest school system in the nation.

The common myth is that the American Indian student population represents all Indian children residing in the United States. Actually, they represent only children of federally recognised tribes living on or near federal reservations or trust lands, and these exist only in the western states. There is only one federally recognised tribe in the eastern states, although there are a few Indian land trusts under state protection. The Mattaponi reservation in Tidewater, Virginia, for example, dates from 1666, a time when Virginia was still a Crown colony of England. Eastern American Indians do not enjoy the status of federally recognised tribes in the west, and are therefore not eligible for federal BIA funds, except those available through public elementary and secondary schools participating in the Indian Education Act programme.

Overall government policy towards Indians, and consequently schools for Indians, has vacillated. Boarding schools for Indians living off reservations were designed to eradicate Indian life and culture.

This policy of divestiture through schooling continued until 1934, when the Roosevelt Administration helped pass the Indian Reorganization Act which made the tribes more autonomous and self-reliant, less dependent on the federal government. Congressional attitude after World War II rescinded these liberalising measures and reverted to the termination of tribes under federal protection. According to this policy, successful tribes were those which indicated a willingness to withdraw altogether from federal services including education programmes. Later, a Kennedy Administration report repudiated this termination policy and emphasised economic and community development, a policy pursued by the Carter Administration.

Partly as a result of the inability of the bureaucracy to respond to Indian schooling needs, contract schools began to emerge in the early 1970s, a century after boarding schools were formed. Contract schools were independent Indian school boards contracting with BIA funds to operate their own school. The money symbolised local control as school names indicate: Rocky Boy, Wind River, Red Cloud, Ramah and Rough Rock. Large cities saw the establishment of Little Big Horn in Chicago, the Milwaukee Urban Indian School and alternative Indian School programmes in big city schools like Seattle and Tacoma.

In 1972 Congress passed the Indian Education Act, the first education legislation for Indians in 50 years. It authorised funds for Indian children attending public schools, not the federally controlled BIA schools. Part A of this Act, also known as the Indian Elementary and Secondary School Assistance Act, redefined the formula for students eligible under impact aid — that programme by which the government compensates local schools for monies not available to them because parents live or work on federal reservations and thereby pay no property taxes. Part B provided money for special educational training programmes for teachers of Indian children and 200 fellowships for selected Indian students for graduate and professional study. Part C established special programmes for adult Indians, mainly from improved literacy opportunities and skills development.

Education programmes for American Indians, however misconceived and mismanaged, constitute one of the oldest federal education projects housed in one of the oldest federal bureaucracies. Its past administration is an example of how the image of federal education can be sullied. It is also an example of how reversible federal education policy can be.

DEPARTMENT OF STATE OVERSEAS SPONSORED SCHOOLS

The US Department of State provides both money and technical assistance to independent overseas schools. There are 148 such schools, operating by locally elected board members, receiving assistance in 88 countries throughout the world. Slightly more than half of the student population are children of parents in the host country or nationals of Third World countries; and a similar proportion of the teachers are American citizens, with the largest number of non-American teachers coming from the host country. The total student population of over 80,000 equals that of a city the size of St Louis. The majority of schools follow the basic American curricular and teaching patterns, and use English as the main medium of instruction. The student body is international in character, and many students are binational and bilingual. Teaching staffs are multinational and multilingual.

The purpose of the Department of State's sponsorship of international schools overseas is not only to provide adequate instructional programmes for elementary and secondary dependents of Americans and to prepare them for American colleges and universities, but also to demonstrate to foreign nationals the philosophy and methods of American educational practices. Although the staff may be multinational, the superintendent or headteacher is always an American. Parents' associations are responsible for electing a board and supervising the superintendent.

However, the schools are not operated or even controlled by the federal government: they are *assisted schools*, and they represent an American interest and investment. They are meant to be characteristic of the best of American educational standards. The schools are thus used as a form of *diplomacy through education* for the international community. They receive the majority of their operating expenses from tuition payments, usually reimbursed by government agencies and business firms, and these are offset by contributions from businesses, local governments, foundations, churches and even a few individuals. Roughly 14 per cent comes from the Department of State's Office of Overseas Schools.

The overseas locale provides quality foreign-language teaching in its academic programme, although the language of the country is not always desired by students or parents. In addition to language study, the school can provide exemplary programmes in history, social studies and the local culture. There is little commercial or vocational education, and the total focus is preparation for college.

TRUST TERRITORY SCHOOLS

The US Department of Interior administers all the US Trust Territories; 2,100 islands. The area is enormous, equal in size to the continental United States; but the land mass is comparatively small, half the size of Rhode Island.

The chequered history of these islands is filled with pages of foreign colonisation. In 1944 a trusteeship was signed with the United Nations giving the US administrative authority over the Marianas, Marshall and Caroline Islands. The Territories also include the Virgin Islands, American Samoa, Guam and all the islands comprising Micronesia. There are a few other scattered islands in the Pacific and one in the Caribbean. Two former states, Alaska and Hawaii, were once territories, as were most western states until full statehood was conferred. Puerto Rico currently has a Commonwealth status.

The Trust Territories conduct most of their own affairs without federal interference. There is a locally functioning legislature, bicameral in nature. The federal government gives assistance for improving the general living conditions of people on the islands, particularly the economy, health and education. The Congress augments the local budget; in many cases, the federal contribution is the lion's share.

. The Micronesian education system follows the standard elementary and secondary school pattern in the United States. There are about 1,500 certified, indigenous teachers, evenly split between those of Micronesian and American origins. The size of the school system is not as significant as its growth rate: at 20 per cent over a three-year period from 1972 to 1975, it was one of the highest in the nation.

The Trust Territories once enjoyed a diversity of post-secondary institutions: the Community College in Ponape, a two-year college specialising in teacher training; the Occupational Center in Palau begun in 1971 with a full range of courses for occupational skills development vital to the Micronesian economy; a maritime training centre in Truk; and a nursing school in Saipan. But in 1977 the Micronesian legislature passed a law establishing the College of Micronesia as a public corporation under a separate board of regents. It combined all these higher education institutions and released the Trust Territory government from administering schools. Most of its curricular programmes prepare students for careers in trades, social services and business in the local economy. The future political status of the Trust Territories is unclear and under negotiation. There are presently several plans for the new form of government.

The Trust Territories have a High Commissioner, but American Samoa has a governor. The seven tropical islands, about 76 square miles (197 km^2) of land, are the only United States possessions south of the equator, over 4,000 (6,500 km) miles from the continental US. American Samoa's public schools are organised into one system, divided into early childhood, elementary, secondary and special education. There are over 800 employees serving about 10,000 students. There are four high schools and 27 elementary schools. The American Samoa Community College has been in existence since 1971 and is fully accredited. It contains an experimental communications satellite terminal whose first course offering was in-service training for nurses beamed from the University of Hawaii over 2,200 miles (3,540 km) away.

The federal government is engaged in administering the schooling of over 300,000 elementary and secondary students, a school population between that of Philadelphia and Chicago, in total the fifth-largest school system in the country. As long as there are Trust Territories, children of American citizens overseas and children of American Indians in Trust, the federal government will always be managing schools.

12

The Politics of Federal Education Organisation

But it will always be easy for the central government, organized as it is in America, to introduce new and more efficacious modes of action, proportioned to its wants.

Alexis de Tocqueville *Democracy in America*

The education service to veterans, college students, the handicapped, the non-English speaking and all those with special interests is federally prompted, in part because of the success of politically active special-interest groups in education, but also because of the void in special programmes in local schools. Lack of money, lack of imagination, lack of leadership, lack of trained personnel all contribute to this schooling malaise. In the long run it is immaterial which level of government supports educational quality. By common consent the nation needs a strengthened education system.

Assuming that a federal legislature and executive will always support education programmes, does it really matter what organisational structure administers such programmes? Educationally, probably not; politically, definitely yes.

The first steps towards a separate Department of Education were in 1926 when President Coolidge told Congress:

I do not favor the making of appropriations from the National Treasury to be expended directly in local education but I do consider it a fundamental requirement of national activity which . . . is worthy of a separate department and a place in the cabinet.

Coolidge felt safe at the time in recommending a Department of Education knowing that Congress would not act on it then or in the near future. He was courting the National Education Association (NEA) and echoing a recommendation that body had made earlier that same year. The NEA Report noted:

In recent decades, the question of the proper relation of the federal government to education has been widely discussed and has received much consideration from Congress . . . [the NEA] would have the national government develop a program of education investigation and research through a Department of Education.

The Department of Education became a reality during the Carter Administration, but there were more opponents, both within and outside the executive branch than there were enthusiasts. The Reagan Administration attempted to dismantle both the Department of Education and the role of the federal government in education. The organisation of federal education has become more political as the role of education in general has become politically radicalised. A brief look at the organisational history is in order.

FEDERAL ORGANISATIONAL BEGINNINGS IN EDUCATION

Rep. James Garfield of Ohio, former Latin and Greek teacher and college president and later to become twentieth President of the United States, argued in the 1860s for the establishment of a 'department of education'. In 1867 President Andrew Jackson signed legislation to the effect that 'there shall be established, at the city of Washington, a department of education'.

Through an appropriation bill, Congress changed the name a year later to the 'Office of Education' at which time it was transferred to the Department of the Interior. Two years later it was renamed the 'Bureau of Education'. Proponents of Education in the 1870s were satisfied that there was some federal activity and were largely unconcerned about its organisational title of affiliation. It was renamed an 'Office' when it was assigned to the Federal Security Agency in 1930.

Henry Barnard became the first US Commissioner of Education in 1867 two weeks after the law creating the 'Department of Education' was signed. This distinguished educator had already been a Connecticut state legislator, the first Superintendent of the common schools for Connecticut, founder of the *Journal of Education*, Chancellor of the University of Wisconsin and President of St John's College in Maryland. He had championed the cause of education in Connecticut as vigorously as had Horace Mann in Massachusetts.

Of his work in the profession, he recalled in later years:

So far back as I have any recollection, the cause of true education — of the complete education of every human being, without regard

173

to the birth or fortune — seemed most worthy of the concentration of all my powers, and, if need be, of any sacrifice of time, money and labor which I might be called upon to make in its behalf. (Barnard)

He stayed only three years in Washington. He had had an appropriated budget, over two years, of $25,000 including his own salary at $4,000, and that of three clerks totalling $5,400. For two years, except for salaries, his real operating expenses were only $6,200. And in his second year in office, 1868, Congress actually reduced his salary by a quarter.

John Eaton brought impressive credentials to the post of Commissioner. A graduate of Dartmouth, he held the commission of a brigadier general and had been a state school superintendent in Tennessee.

President Grant appointed Eaton, who served as Commissioner from 1870 to 1886. His long tenure testified to his administrative success with Congress, the staff expanded tenfold to 38, and the library holdings increased from 100 to 1,800 volumes. Eaton served under Presidents Grant, Hayes, Garfield, Arthur and Cleveland — one of the longest tenures of any senior education official.

In spite of the efforts of Eaton and his successors, and the many, apparently meaningless changes in the title, the role of federal education remained a backwater concern. The principal responsibility was to collect statistics and generate reports on progress by the state, reports which gained some credibility but were mostly ignored.

THE US OFFICE OF EDUCATION IN TRANSITION

From its beginning in 1867 until 1962, federal education was not the marketplace for competing public philosophies about federalism and public policy in education. Even under Commissioner Sterling McMurrin, appointed by President Kennedy, the Office of Education had only three bureaux: research and development, international education (nearly totally dominated by the personnel and programmes of the Department of State and Agency for International Development) and educational assistance. The education specialists saw themselves as technical advisors to programmes in the states, a realistic extension of the service philosophy. Change was inevitable. It came suddenly and traumatically. Keppel, appointed in 1962 specifically to bring change to the agency, was not in the tradition of former education leaders, and he saw his role as that of strategist to a very reluctant and lethargic system. His strategy was to await the outcome of impending legislation, for he knew that this would help determine the structure of the US Office of Education of organisation.

The months of July through September, 1965, were painful, not to say traumatic for the entire agency. But if they witnessed the wrecking of an old house, they also saw the creation of the foundations for a new one. Structural reorganization was important — less as an instrument to improve administrative rationality in some abstract sense than as a device for establishing new priorities. (Bailey and Mosher, 1968)

The passage of the Elementary and Secondary Education Act changed forever the operation of the Office of Education. The technical service function became subsumed in the administration of categorical programmes.

Prior to the Eisenhower Administration, the Office of Educaion had been a part organisationally of the Federal Security Agency. It was hidden, unobtrusive, without funding authority, and publishing only an occasional booklet. Then, during the Eisenhower Administration came explosive post-World War II social programmes, and the creation of the Department of Health Education and Welfare (HEW) in 1953. Over the years HEW brought a new national commitment to a social agenda where little had existed before. At its height, its 350 separate programmes affected half the population. Its budget at one time was 36 per cent of the total for the government. It once employed 150,000 people.

By 1967 the US Office of Education, still a part of HEW, was characterised by the size of its budget relative to its organisational structure within a department. In the late 1960s it was responsible for a dollar appropriaton of $4 billion, larger than all other federal departments except defence. Education had the money, the programmes and the personnel; it did not have a cabinet spokesperson.

THE US DEPARTMENT OF EDUCATION

Carter, campaigning in 1976, promised a separate Department of Education, while also voicing concern for the proliferation of federal programmes.

175

I'm in favor of creating a separate Cabinet level Department of Education. Generally, I'm opposed to the proliferation of federal agencies . . . But the Department of Education would consolidate the grant programs, job training, early childhood education, literacy training, and many other functions currently scattered throughout the government. The result would be a stronger voice for education at the federal level. (Califano, 1982)

A Department was by now a political promise with a 50-year history. However there were real differences. Whereas Coolidge had been interested only in a small agency with no federal funds, Carter was committed to reducing the size of government. The establishment of a Department was only a part of his plan for total government reduction and co-ordination. During the 1976 campaign he made repeated assurances that he was going to reduce the number of agencies from 1,900 to 200.

The proposal for a separate Department of Education was not merely contained in a random political speech or a legislative or presidential whim. It had been afoot since the turn of the century. A Report of a Special Subcommittee on Education for the 90th Congress (1975) notes: 'For at least six decades a proposal for a Cabinet-level Department of Education has been before the Congress in one form or another.'

The principal opposition came from the American Federation of Teachers (AFT), whose main argument was that the creation of a new Department would isolate education in the federal bureaucracy, thus making it more vulnerable to special-interest groups. Moreover, the higher education community, fearing that its constituency would be short-changed and lose out to the elementary and secondary schooling interest, also strongly opposed the creation of a new Department. This opposition continued even though many higher education funds came through Office of Education programmes: via, for example, the National Science Foundation, the National Institute of Health and Mental Health. Strong opposition also came from advocates of non-public education, notably from the Catholic Education Association. There was fear that private and parochial schools would lose what little funds were available.

The principal foci of opposition to a new Department, political expectations and legal ambiguities aside, were arguments over federal interference and control over local education policies and practices. Categorical programmes in education were associated in the public consciousness with the growing image of the welfare state. Education, under the structure of HEW, shared that disreputable image: of ordinary taxpayers digging deeper for the freeloaders.

Again, the federal statute was clear on what could not be done. The General Education Provisions Act (1977) states:

> No provision of [and here follows a listing of all Education congressional acts] shall be construed to authorize any department, agency, officer, or employee of the United States to exercise any direction, supervision, or control over curriculum, program of instruction, administration, or personnel of any education institution, school or school system, or over the selection of library resources, textbooks, or other printed or published instructional materials by any education institution or school system, or to require the assignment or transportation of students or teachers in order to overcome racial imbalance.

For those who accept the federal funds, regulations, auditors and advisors are not always equally welcomed. However, where goes federal money, there also goes control over the money.

Joseph Califano, Carter's Secretary of HEW, initially did not realise how committed his President was to a separate Department of Education. Califano had in fact in his writings opposed the move, and was on record as favouring some federal assistance to higher education, but a diminished role for federal assistance to elementary and secondary education. He believed that the Congress had become too receptive and pliant to individual education-interest groups and had proliferated too many categorical programmes. Programme examples included metric education, ethnic studies, consumer education, women's equity, environmental education, library programmes and Indian education. These education-related categories were narrow, in some cases partisan, congressional responses that demonstrated the power of the interest groups. Often, these groups got from Congress what they could not get from local school boards or state legislatures.

Califano was one of the key political education apointees in the Carter Administration. He had been a policy developer and bureaucrat, having served under Robert McNamara in the Department of Defense during the Kennedy Administration and as President Johnson's executive domestic policy assistant in the White House for domestic affairs. He was the last HEW Secretary. He left disappointed, as he explains:

177

I came to HEW enthusiastic about the opportunity to improve education in America, and determined to step up federal funding sharply. I left alarmed over the deterioration of public education in America and troubled by the threat to academic freedom that the federal role, enlarged and shaped by special interests, poses. (Califano, 1982)

Califano was basically opposed to a new Department of Education. He was opposed managerially — he did not think it would provide improved administration of education — and he did not want to give the message that the federal government was going to involve itself more in education. However, his most important reason was that he felt that the integrity of higher education, its academic freedom and creative independence would be in jeopardy, threatened by the increased federal presence. He conveyed all these misgivings to President Carter.

Clearly, the proposal for a separate Department of Education at a time when the statistics revealed a decline in a national test score, when there was a rise in urban and school violence, illiteracy and school vandalism, was not going to help solve the nation's educational depression. Even Carter's Office of Management and Budget arrived at a similar conclusion and issued a report opposing the creating of such a Department.

Yet in his State of the Union address on 19 January 1978, Carter committed himself to a Department. After that the fight was on to see which programmes would be transferred, and from what departments and agencies. The Carter Administration wanted to avoid battles within the Administration. Aides hastened to reassure the veterans' groups, for example, that their programmes would not be included. Even the NEA wanted a narrow focus for the proposed Department, one that included little more than already existed in the Office of Education.

One controversial area was that of student loans and grants. There were more than 50 schemes throughout the government, only a few of which were in the education division at the time. A comprehensive management scheme would have included them all, conveniently consolidating them under an umbrella agency. It had already been done in Califano's HEW. But it never happened in Carter's Department, and a unique opportunity was lost, which, if it had been seized, would have saved millions of dollars in administrative duplication, the very rationale for the proposed Department.

One by one, programmes proposed were left untouched in the

reorganisation as Carter tested the political waters with caution, and vacillated. Special-education interest groups, both within and outside the federal bureaucracy, manoeuvred to keep their enterprises intact. Senator Ribicoff's Senate Government Affairs Committee felt the pressure. Soon veterans' educational programmes were exempted from transfer to the new department, then Head Start, school lunch and milk programmes from the Department of Agriculture, and the Bureau of Indian Affairs schools from the Department of the Interior. The transfer of the Department of Defense Overseas schools was postponed. When the legislation was finally enacted in the spring of 1979 and the new Department established, it was a triumph for political expediency over boldness and decisiveness.

The effectiveness of educational advocacy was diminished in the Carter Administration. The structure of a federal agency, not the importance of education, became the central issue. There was not even the rhetoric of schooling improvement.

The Reagan Administration's first paramount education platform was the elimination of the new department as a signal of Conservatism's reduction of the federal role for education. However, towards the end of his first term, Reagan was persuaded to turn his considerable media skills on behalf of education and to forget its bureaucratic structure. He himself became an education advocate, to the astonishment of his critics, and largely ignored the House that Carter built.

CONCLUSION

Understanding the federal government's role in education is an exercise in understanding the workings of democratic government in America. Thus, political slogans which have urged the citizen to eliminate federal participation in education reveal an ignorance of the long federal presence in educational history. Efforts to reduce the amount of federal involvement, except for the judiciary, will follow cyclically from previous expansionary trends. The right of the federal government to enter into schooling policies and practices is constitutionally unambiguous within all three branches: executive, legislative and judicial.

Each past federal action by Congress has been a response to a national crisis or to a selected student population. The segregation of schools, the handicapped, busing, student loans, bilingual education, libraries — each categorical aid programme has sought to remedy a local or state education deficiency, or to upgrade a national priority. Recipients of federal programmes rarely complain.

Nevertheless, throughout the Reagan Administration there was a favourable response to reducing an unseemly aggregation of federal programmes whose accumulated presence, in spite of congressional good intentions, proved to be more of a local schooling burden than a blessing. The concept of the federal government's excessive control in education, popular in the 1960s and 1970s, had given way to hard economic necessities. The federal deficit was growing exponentially, and all government programmes had to be reduced. For the Reagan Administration this was already the principal domestic political ideology.

The view that less federal influence and control somehow means more control in local schools and in states ignores the role of the judiciary. Federal courts extended constitutional rights to clients of education who had not previously had access to educational opportunities and privileges. The 1983 US Supreme Court decision *Plyles vs Doe*, which held as unconstitutional the exclusion of children of illegal aliens, is a case in point. It is a sign of the continued intervention in local education affairs. This one decision has substantially altered funding allocations in schools with sizeable populations of alien families, particularly in southern states. It could be that states and local schools could argue for greater federal financial assistance, as schools did for desegregation assistance, as a direct result of this court decision.

Although educational policy-making by the federal judiciary has waned since the 1960s and 1970s, its power to regulate and enforce, and to reaffirm constitutionally protected rights in education, has been well established. Individuals could well turn to the courts to stimulate congressional or executive action in the future.

The consolidation of federal aid programmes, especially the Education Consolidation and Improvement Act (ECIA) reduced 28 programmes to one block grant to the states. Preliminary evaluation of programme effectiveness revealed that the Act succeeded in reducing the amount of administration, particularly the paperwork.

Does reduction of paperwork, however, lead to more effective schooling practices on behalf of those selected student populations that federal programmes serve, like the handicapped? An alternative structure for federal aid to schools, as Ginsburg and Turnbull (1981) argue, could be improved local programme co-ordination.

Although the Reagan Administration radically curtailed federal funding for education and consolidated discrete, categorical aid programmes, the President did in fact ascend a pulpit and argue the cause of education. He spoke at length on education, on what Kaplan (1984) described as: 'a magpie's nest of such issues as excellence, good teaching, morality, restoration of parental authority, prayers in the schools, a return to basics, and stringent measures to combat drug and alcohol abuse'. This may sound like a string of political catchwords, merely using the theme of education, to capture the voting public; but it took the wind out of the sails of the opposition, and lent executive leadership to the problems of education.

The publication in 1983 of *A Nation at Risk* energised public opinion about schooling concerns. In clear and unequivocal language the report spoke of lowered achievement, poor salaries for teachers, uninspired curricula, a new need for mathematics and science. Reagan did not agree with many of the recommendations, because they presumed a federal response, but he keenly sensed the nation's mood for improvement. No one could have predicted that a report from a task force emanating from a demoralised Department of Education on a subject low on everyone's federal priority would have a distribution of three million copies. Public interest in education was high, and it turned the Reagan Administration into a fierce education advocate.

Predicting what the federal role in education should be is hazardous guesswork, but perhaps not much riskier than the work of the weatherman or the economist. Let me venture my presumptions:

- The congressional and executive branches should support mainly higher education activities, for both institutions and individuals, and abandon elementary and secondary education support, leaving that to states and localities.
- The congressional and executive branches should promote early childhood programmes, especially nutrition, for pre-elementary children and their mothers as a way of preparing a healthy child for entering elementary schooling.
- The congressional and executive branches, with assistance from the judiciary, should support every individual's right to participate on an equal basis in any educational service.
- The congressional and executive branches should provide limited but consistent support for research, demonstration and assessment activities of American education and disseminate these findings as widely as possible.
- All branches of government should continue to support American Indian education, as this clearly has always been in law and in fact a federal responsibility.

- The Congress should intervene with support for public education only in the most serious and critical national emergency, and then only for a specific amount of time, and never as a funded entitlement.
- The Congress should begin the process of formalising a constitutional amendment specifying everyone's right to a free public elementary and secondary education, a present serious omission in our constitutional provisions and freedoms.

Whatever the emerging federal role, educational policy at all levels will have to contend with the problems of equalising school financial allocations, desegregating schools, providing access for disadvantaged handicapped and minority children, and satisfying public demands for improved quality — all with reduced funding. The wide range of challenges to schools — because of shrinking enrolments, lowered teacher quality, the shift to private education, and decline in test scores — may prompt different kinds of federal responses.

I began this study of the federal role in education by pointing out that the educational history of support and participation is traceable back to the founding of the American democracy. That tradition is young compared with some European republics, but the principles of participation from all sectors of the population, of representation and of established law must not be allowed to erode or dissipate. Though the emergent nations have often initially modelled themselves on the West, democratic life in much of Asia and Africa is fragile and subject to totalitarianism and external intervention. Democracy is not an absolute or guaranteed form of government that endures in spite of the vigilance of its citizens. Schooling in democracy, however cliché-worn the phrase, is education's chief mission.

Those who began constitutional democracy in America were men of wide vision and learning, developing ideas which knowledgeable observers described as radical in government and revolutionary in thought. But the people of late eighteenth-century America, for and by whom republican government was founded, were generally not knowledgeable, not even literate. Nevertheless, these constitutional executors believed that citizens had to become better informed in order to preserve the form and substance of the government they and their posterity would inherit. Education, in part aided by federal government leadership and resources, is a partnership in preserving that unique heritage.

Select Bibliography

Bailey, Stephen and Edith Mosher (1968) *The Office of Education Administers a Law*, Ithaca, New York, Syracuse University Press

Beames, John (1961) *Memoirs of a Bengal Civilian*, London, Chatto & Windus

Belton vs Gebhart (1952) Dover, Delaware, Supreme Court of Delaware

Berger, Raoul (1979) *Government by Judiciary, The Transformation of the Fourteenth Amendment*, Cambridge, Mass., Harvard University Press

Bishop, Joseph Bucklin (1919) *Theodore Roosevelt's Letters to His Children*, New York, Charles Scribner's & Sons

Boyd, Julian P. (1955) *The Papers of Thomas Jefferson*, Princeton, New Jersey, Princeton University Press

Brant, Irving (1965) *The Bill of Rights, Its Origin and Meaning*, Indianapolis, Indiana, Bobbs & Merrill

Brown vs Board of Education (1954) 347 US 483

Califano, Joseph (1982) *Governing America*, New York, Touchstone Books

Cooper vs Aaron (1958) 358 US 1

Crawford vs Board of Education, City of Los Angeles (1981) 458 US 527

De Toqueville, Alexis (1969) *Democracy in America*, New York, Doubleday

Durant, W. (1934) *The Life of Greece*, New York, Simon and Shuster

Fenno, Richard (1985) *Congress in Change, Evolution and Reform*, Washington, DC, American Enterprise Institute

Finn, Chester (1977) *Education and the Presidency*, Lexington, Mass., Lexington Books

Folks, Homer (1900) *The Care of Destitute, Neglected and Delinquent Children*, New York, The Chanties Review

Ferguson, John H. and Dean E. McHenry (1950) *The American Federal Government*, New York, McGraw Hill

Franklin, Benjamin (1970) *The Complete Poor Richard Almanacs*, vol. I, Barre, Mass., Imprint Society

Gaines vs Canada (1938) V. 305, US 337

Ginsburg, Alan L. and Brenda Turnbull (1981) 'Local Program Coordination: An Alternative Structure for Federal Aid to Schools', *Educational Evaluation and Policy Analysis*, vol. 3, no. 3

Hawke, D.F. (1971) *Benjamin Rush: Revolutionary Gadfly*, Indianapolis, Bobbs & Merrill

Hawkins v Board of Control of Florida (1956) V. 350, US 413

Hoover, Herbert (1952) *The Memoirs of Herbert Hoover*, vol. II, New York, Macmillan

Indian Education: A National Tragedy, A National Challenge (1969), Washington DC, US Government Printing Office

Johnson, Lyndon Baines (1971) *Vantage Point, Perspectives of the Presidency, 1963-69*, New York, Holt, Rinehart & Winston

Kaplan, George R. (1984) 'Hail to a Chief or Two: The Indifferent Presidential Record in Education', *Phi Delta Kappan*, September

Kennedy, R. (1971) *Thirteen Days, A Memoir of the Cuban Missile Crisis*, New York, Norton

Koenig, R.A. (1978) 'The Law and Education in Historical Perspective' in *The Courts and Education*, Chicago, University of Chicago Press

Locke, John (1964) *Some Thoughts Concerning Education*, London, Heineman

Malbin, M. (1980) *Unelected Representatives: Congressional Staff and the Future of Representative Government*, New York, Basic Books

Mayer, J. and A.P. Kerr (eds), *Democracy in America* by Alexis de Tocqueville, New York, Doubleday

McLaurin vs Oklahoma State Regents for Higher Education, (1950) V. 339, US 637

Mill, John Stuart (1961) 'On Representative Government' in *Essential Works*, New York, Bantam Books

Milliken vs Bradley (1974) US 717 ('Milliken I')

Myrdal, G. (1944) *An American Dilemma: The Negro Problem and Modern Democracy*, New York, Harper Bros

Nation At Risk, A (1983), Washington, DC, US Government Printing Office

Plessey vs Ferguson (1896) 163, US 537

Plyles vs Doe (1981) 458 US 1131

Revel, Jean Francois (1971) *Without Marx or Jesus*, New York, Doubleday

Rockefeller, John D. (1973) *The Second American Revolution*, New York, Harper & Row

Ruttand, Robert, A. *et al.* (1977) *The Federalist Papers of James Madison* (v. 10), Chicago, University of Chicago Press

San Antonio vs Rodriguez (1973) 411, US 1

Sawer, C. (1975) *The Australian Constitution*, Canberra, Australian Government Printing Service

Servan-Schreiber, J.J. (1979) *The American Challenge*, Boston, Atheneum

Stanley, David (1964) *The Higher Civil Service, An Evaluation of Federal Personnel Practices*, Washington, DC, The Brookings Institution

Suffian, T.M. (1975) *An Introduction to the Constitution of Malaysia*, Kuala Lumpur, Government Printing Office

Summerfield, Harry L. (1974) *Power and Process, The Formation and Limits of Federal Educational Policy*, Berkeley, McCutchan

Sweatt vs Painter (1949) V. 339, US 629

Swann vs Charlotte-Mecklenberg (1971) 402, US 1

Tiedt, Sidney W. (1966) *The Role of the Federal Government in Education*, New York, Oxford University Press

Toffler, A. (1970) *Future Shock*, New York, Random House

Tyack, David (1970) 'New Perspectives on the History of American Education' in Herbert J. Bass (ed.), *The State of American History*, 22-42, Chicago, Quadrangle Books

Washington vs Seattle City School District (1981) 458, US 457

Webster, Noah (1962) *American Spelling Book*, New York, Teachers College, Columbia University

White House Conference 1930 (1931) New York, The Century Co.

Wills, Garry (1978) *Inventing America*, New York, Doubleday

Wills, Garry (1980) *Explaining America, The Federalist*, New York, Doubleday

Wilson, Woodrow (1889) *The State, Elements of Historical and Practical Politics*, Boston, DC Heath

Index

Adams, John 62
admission and race 72ff.
Adult Education Act 134
Agnew, Spiro, Vice Pres. 134
Alaska 71, 170
Albany, New York 69
Alien and Sedition Act 59, 165
Allen, James A., Comm. 135,
   143, 155
Anglicans 30
American Federation of Teachers
   175
American Indians 13, 15, 16,
   71, 163, 165ff., 181
Aristotle 89
Armed Forces Staff College 165
Arthur, Chester A., Pres. 126
Articles of Confederation 10, 13,
   14, 20, 61, 98
Atomic Energy Commission 158
Australia 12
   Constitution of 45ff.

Baker, Howard, Sen. 137
Barnard, Henry, Comm. 173
Barron vs Baltimore 65
Basic Educational Opportunity
   Grants (Pell grants) 157
Beames, John 154
Bell, Ted, Sec. 141, 146, 155
Belton vs Gebhart 75
Berger, Raoul 65
Bill of Rights (1st Amendment)
   109, 121
Blacks 13
block grant 180
Boston, Massachusetts 69
Boucher, Jonathan, Revd 12
Brademas, John, Rep. 104, 111
Britain (British) 13, 15, 16, 17,
   24, 28, 33, 121
British North America Act
   (1867) 43
Brooke, Robert, Gov. 28
Brown vs Board of Education

(1954) 68, 76, 77ff.
Brown, Henry B., Justice 74
Buchanan, James, Pres. 124
Bureau of Indian Affairs 165,
   166, 179
bureaucrats, bureaucracy, federal
   158ff., 160
Burger, Chief Justice 84
Burke, Thomas 13, 18
busing 112, 144, 179
   race and state power 80ff.

Califano, Joseph, Sec. 144, 177,
   178
California 68, 81
California Supreme Court 80
Canada 12
   Constitution of 43ff.
Carr, William 151
Carter, Jimmie, Pres. 5, 136,
   144, 149, 155, 175, 178
   Administration 102, 111,
   122, 137ff., 146, 168, 172,
   177, 179
categorical programmes 158,
   159, 177, 179, 180-1
Catholic Education Association
   175
certiorari 61
Charles I 16, 90
civil rights 143
Civil Rights Act (1866, 1964)
   80, 94, 98-9, 134, 143, 145,
   154
civil servants 158ff.
Civil Service Commission 158
Civil War 59, 96
Civilian Conservation Corps
   (CCC, 1937) 163
Cleveland, Grover, Pres. 123,
   126
Code of Federal Regulations 156
Coleman Report 145
Colonial Laws of Validity Act
   (1865) 46

185